OPTIONS
TRADING
STRATEGIES

A step by step guide for online trading in stock market and foreign exchange whit great ideas analysis and strategies for passive income plan whit an ultimate trading flatforms thats can have best outcome

By Michael Swing

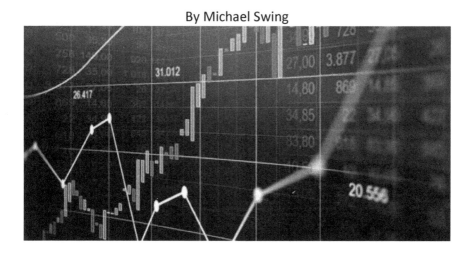

Text Copyright © [Michael Swing]

Legal & Disclaimer

The information contained in this book and its contents is not designed to replace or take the place of any form of medical or professional advice; and is not meant to replace the need for independent medical, financial, legal or other professional advice or services, as may be required. The content and information in this book has been provided for educational and entertainment purposes only.

The content and information contained in this book has been compiled from sources deemed reliable, and it is accurate to the best of the Author's knowledge, information and belief. However, the Author cannot guarantee its accuracy and validity and cannot be held liable for any errors and/or omissions. Further, changes are periodically made to this book as and when needed. Where appropriate and/or necessary, you must consult a professional (including but not limited to your doctor, attorney, financial advisor or such other professional advisor) before using any of the suggested remedies, techniques, or information in this book.

Upon using the contents and information contained in this book, you agree to hold harmless the Author from and against any damages, costs, and expenses, including any legal fees potentially resulting from the application of any of the information provided by this book. This disclaimer applies to any loss, damages or injury caused by the use and application, whether directly or indirectly, of any advice or information presented, whether for breach of contract, tort, negligence, personal injury, criminal intent, or under any other cause of action.

You agree to accept all risks of using the information presented inside this book.

You agree that by continuing to read this book, where appropriate and/or necessary, you shall consult a professional (including but not limited to your doctor, attorney, or financial advisor or such other advisor as needed) before using any of the suggested remedies, techniques, or information in this book.

Table of Contents

OPTIONS TRADING STRATEGIES

Introduction

A lot of investors only know about bonds, stocks, and mutual funds. Actually, there are so many types of investments that investors can put their money into. An option is one type of investment which offers a different kind of opportunity to experienced investors.

An option is very versatile because it allows an investor to adjust or adapt his position depending on the present situation. It can be conservative or speculative depending on the investing style of the investor. It means that he can protect his position depending on the market movement. However, the versatility of an option has its downside. An option is very complex and very risky. As such, a disclaimer is often issued by brokers when an investor wants to try options trading. Therefore, only serious investors are encouraged to try it. He must spend time studying options before he tries trading them. Thus, this book is a good start to learn about the trade.

An option is actually an agreement between the buyer and seller. The buyer is under no obligation to transact the underlying asset before the option expiry at a specific price. However, he has the right to demand the completion of the agreement. An option is a binding contract with strict definition of properties and terms. It a type of derivatives with an index or stock as the most common underlying asset used.

Types of Options

There are 2 kinds of options: call and put. A call option is a contract which provides the buyer the right to buy an underlying asset before it expires at a pre-agreed price. In stock trading, a call is like taking a long position. In this contract, the buyer is hoping that the price of the underlying asset will increase before the call option expires. A put option, on the other hand, is a right to sell an underlying asset before the contract expires and at a specific price. In stock trading, this is equivalent to taking a short position. A buyer of a put option hopes that the price of the asset goes down before the option expires.

Options can also be American or European. An American option is an option which can be exercised even before it expires. In general, an exchange-traded option is an American option. A European option is an option which can only be exercised on the date of expiration. A long term option is known as LEAPS or long term equity anticipation security. In terms of managing and controlling risk, LEAPS is similar to a regular option. However, LEAPS offer opportunities for a longer time. An exotic option is a non-standard option.

Stakeholders in an Options Market

There are 4 types of traders in an options market: buyer of call option, seller of call option, buyer of put option, and seller of put option. A person who purchases an option is called a holder while the one who sells it is called a writer. Just like in stocks, an investor who buys an option takes a long position while the one who sells it takes a short position.

In both options, a holder has no obligation to consummate the option contract. However, he has the right to either buy or sell the underlying asset if he wants to. Furthermore, a writer has an obligation to deliver his promise to either buy or sell the underlying asset if the holder exercises his right.

The Terminologies in Options Trading

The strike price is the price of the underlying asset which can either be sold or purchased. If it's a call option, the holder will make a profit when the market price of the underlying assets goes above the strike price. He can exercise the option if he wants to realize the profit. Otherwise, he can let it expire. On the other hand, if it's a put option, the writer will make a profit if the market price falls below the strike price. He can exercise the option if he wants to take advantage of the profit.

A listed option is an option which is traded through an options exchange. In the United States of America, options trader uses the Chicago Board Options Exchange to trade options. A listed option has an expiration date and a fixed strike price. Furthermore, 1 contract constitutes 100 shares of the underlying asset.

A call option is said to be "in the money" if the market price is above the strike price. In a put option, "in the money" means that the market price of the underlying asset is below the strike price. Intrinsic value is the "in the money" amount. The premium is the price paid for the option. It includes factors like volatility, strike price, market price of the underlying asset, and the time value of the option prior to expiration. The process of computing the option premium is very complex.

How Options Work

Why Trade Options

An investor can use options either to hedge or to speculate. In options trading, an investor can make a profit even if the market is down. In fact, he can even make money if the market moves sideways. This is the type of versatility that option trading offers.

Speculation is a trading strategy wherein a person can earn or lose a lot of money. It is because of this that trading options is considered very risky. If an investor buys an option, he has to correctly determine the time, the magnitude, and the direction of the underlying asset's price. He must be able to predict correctly the direction of the price. He must be correct about the time frame and the amount of change in the price. Plus, he has to consider that he has to pay commissions to the broker. As such, the investor has to beat all these odds in order to make money. He uses leveraging to earn a great deal of money.

Hedging is like insurance. He insures his investments in case their values fall. Large institutions actually use hedging because these establishments find it useful. Even an individual person can take advantage of hedging opportunities offered by the options market. For example, he wants to invest in technology stocks. However, he doesn't want to lose a lot of money from his stock investment. Thus, he can use options in order to limit his losses while taking advantage of the full opportunity offered by the technology stocks.

A third reason, although not available to everyone, allows a lot of companies to entice and keep their best employees through an employee stock option, which is similar to a regular option which provides the right to the holder to buy the company stock. The contract is between the company and its employee. In a regular option, the contract can be any two parties.

How Option Trading Works

For example, Company A has a stock price of $50 and a premium of $3.15 on May 1 for a July 53 Call. This means that the expiry date is on the **3rd** Friday of July and the strike price is $53. The contract price is $315 ($3.15 x 100 shares). Commissions are ignored in this example although in reality, the trader has to account for commissions.

The trader hopes that the stock rise will go up above $53 so that he'll make a profit. The break-even price for this contract is $53.15. The option is worthless when the stock price is $50 because it's less than the strike price of $53. After 2 weeks, the stock price went up to $61. The options contract is now worth $825. The profit will be $510 ($825 - $315). Therefore, in just 2 weeks, the investor is able to double his money. He can close his position by selling his option so that he can realize his profits or he can maintain his position if he thinks that the stock price will still go up. If at expiry date the stock price falls to $45, he can let it expire worthless and lose his original investment of $315 because the stock price is less than the strike price.

In reality, just 10% of these options are exercised. 30% of options are left to expire worthless and the rest is traded out. Holders of options sell their positions before expiry and the writers by them to close their positions.

In the example, the option premium increased from $3.15 to $8.25. Time value and intrinsic value made it possible for the premium to increase. Basically, the premium is the sum of the time value and intrinsic value. Intrinsic value is the in-the-money amount. In a call option, it is that point where the strike price is equal to the stock price. The time value, on the other hand, is the possibility that the option will increase in value. Therefore, in the example, the $8 is the intrinsic value while $0.25 is the time value. In general, an option always trade more than the underlying asset's intrinsic value.

Where to Buy Options

In the United States of America, options contracts are traded in different options exchanges. A trader must sign up with an options broker to be able to trade options. The orders to the broker are then routed to the options exchange. There are brokers who allow the trader to choose where to route his order while most brokers have their standardized way of choosing the exchange where the order is carried out.

Before trading options, the broker will first have to approve the trader's level of options trading. The trader has to fill out an options form which is used by the broker to evaluate the trading strategies as well as the level of understanding of options of the trader. In addition, the trader's general experience on investing is also evaluated. A broker has at most 5 levels of approval and includes factors like account balance, investing history, and investing objectives.

A trader's level may be conservative or aggressive. He is given options strategies by the broker depending on his options trading level. He may not be allowed to use riskier strategies if these involve a lot of risk. An experience trader with more liquid assets may be assigned a higher approval level than a person with a smaller account and less experience. After assigning an options trading level, the trader can start using the trading platform offered by the broker. He can start scanning positions which fit his trading strategy or market outlook. He can start submitting orders through the trading platform or through the phone.

There are less popular ways of routing orders. An over-the-counter option isn't transacted in an exchange. It is a contract between 2 independent parties. The disadvantage of an over-the-counter option is that it isn't regulated by the Options Clearing Corporation unlike the exchange-traded options. In general, only investors with large investments and institutional traders use over-the-counter options.

Reading The Options Table

Because of data dissemination and electronic trading, more and more traders are taking advantage of the benefits of trading options. Some use options to hedge while some traders try to speculate on the direction of the market price. There are also those traders who are still in the process of learning how to profit from the trade. Whatever their reason, they can be successful if they choose the right option. Currently, an option trader has a lot of resources available to him unlike traders in the past.

In previous years, newspapers report option price by a list of rows which is difficult to decipher. Today, some newspapers still use that old format of reporting option data. The reports usually consisted of notations like "P" or "C" to indicate a put or a call option. It also includes the last option trade price and the strike price. Some lists include open interest and volume figures. These figures are considered passé by most savvy option traders who understand various factors that can move options trading.

Today, options traders rely on online sources for option data. Although most sources have their own formats in the presentation of data, there are important variables that are present in each of the report. The OpSym in the first column of most reports include the symbol of the underlying asset, the contract month and year, the strike price, as well as the "p" or "c" notation to indicate a put or call option. The second column is the "bid" price, which is the most recent price a market maker offers to purchase a specific option. It means that a writer can make an order to sell a particular option contract at its bid price. The **3rd** column is the ask price which is the most recent price a holder can buy a particular option contract.

It is important to note that market makers earn a living from the "bid" and "ask" prices. An option trader must compute the difference between the 2 prices before he considers entering or exiting a position. Usually, if the option is actively traded, it has a tighter spread (the difference between the bid and ask prices which is also the market maker's commission). If the spread is wide, it can cause a lot of problems to the short term trader because he can lose money even if he makes a profit.

The fourth column is the extrinsic bid/ask, which is the time premium that the option price has currently built. This information is important because ultimately all options lose their time premium at expiry date. The **5th** column is the implied volatility bid/ask. It is computed using a pricing model like the Black-Scholes model. It is the expected level of future volatility based on the option's current price and other variables used in computing volatility. A high implied volatility means that the option price has built more time premium. If the option trader can avail of historical implied volatility values, he can find out if the present extrinsic value is on a high or low level. If the extrinsic value is on a high level, the option is best for sellers. On the other hand, if it's low, it means that buyers can benefit most from the option.

The sixth column is the delta bid/ask, which is computed using a pricing model and represents the equivalent position of the underlying asset. The value can range from 0 to 100 for a call option and 0 to -100 for a put option. For example, if the delta is computed to be 50, it means that the risk/reward of the call option is the same as owning 50 shares of the underlying asset. If the underlying asset goes up by 1 point, the option can rise about 0.5 point. If the delta value is near 100, it means that the option is trading more like its underlying stock. The gamma bid/ask is on the **7th** column. The value is also derived using a pricing model. It shows the number of deltas an option can gain or lose if the underlying stock gains a point. For example, a holder has a March 2015 125 call at $3.50. The delta will be 58.20, which means that if the value of the underlying stock goes up by $1 the option will gain about $0.5820. If the gamma value is computed to be 5.65 deltas, the delta will be 63.85 (58.20 + 5.65). This means that if the price of the underlying asset goes up by $1, the option gain will be about $0.6385.

The eighth column is the Vega bid/ask, which shows the amount that the option price can possibly rise or fall based on a 1 point increase in implied volatility. If the implied volatility goes up by a point, then in the example above the option price will gain $0.141. It is better to purchase an option if it has low implied volatility. On the other hand, it is better to sell an option if it has high implied volatility. The 9th column is the theta bid/ask, which the amount by which the option may fall due to the passage of a day. Because as was noted in the 4th column, as the option nears expiration, it loses it time premium. Furthermore, as the expiration draws near, the option loses it time value faster.

The tenth column is the volume which shows the number of contracts trader for the specific option as per the latest session. In general, a high volume option has a tighter bid/ask spread. The **11th** column is the open interest which shows the number of open contracts of a specific option. The last column is the strike price, which the option price a buyer can pay for the underlying asset if he decides to exercise the option. It is also the price the seller will sell the underlying asset if the option is exercised by his buyer.

A call option has a higher option price if the strike price is lower. On the other hand, a put option is more expensive if the strike price is higher. Furthermore, a cap option has a positive delta while a put option has a negative delta.

Chapter 1: Managing Option Positions

Rolling positions

What is rolling?

Sometimes options traders wish to make adjustments to positions they hold in the market. When this happens, it means the trader's market outlook has changed. It is actually possible to roll a short or long option position.

The term rolling refers to changing the outlook on the underlying security of an option. This change is often driven by a change in the outlook of the markets and positions held on certain trades. In such situations, a trader is often worried that certain positions will be assigned.

Rolling is similar to making a different turn other than the one initially planned. Think, for instance, you leave home heading to the grocery store only to end up at the movies. This is very similar to what rolling is about.

The aim of rolling is to either deter or cancel the assignment. Basically, managing positions through rolling is an advanced technique that should only be applied by seasoned traders and experienced investors. Therefore, as an intermediate trader, you need to ensure that you thoroughly understand this process before applying it.

Rolling a position

Anytime that a trader rolls a position, he or she will be purchasing options very close to a current position in the marketing then sell this position in order to start another one. This process will cause small, minute but significant tweaks to the strike prices of options held by the trader. The effect of this move will be to shift the expiration times further out, so positions do not expire as initially planned. Even then, this process is not a guarantee that the strategy will work. In extreme cases, rolling will only compound losses, so it is advisable that only experienced traders apply this technique.

1. How to Roll a Covered Call

When you hold covered calls, you can choose to sell them in order to reduce the cost of holding them in long positions. When rolling calls forward, you will improve the break-even position and make it easier to be successful in the long run. However, you need to know if a position should be rolled on and when to do so. For instance, should rolling of a position occur 20 days to expiration or possibly at expiration?

Also, just about any trader can write a covered call. The most crucial thing is to manage such a position appropriately. Certain factors should be considered when rolling a position especially near expiration Fridays.

First, you need to confirm whether the underlying stock is suitable for this kind of management. Then you will need to confirm the option chains for statistics involving current and next month.

Now use the Ellman Calculator and enter the statistics in order to determine whether the dates are viable for rolling management. The 1-month goal for initial returns stands at 2% to 4%. With this information, you will finally need to conduct a thorough evaluation chart technical information and the prevailing market conditions. This way, you will comfortably be able to make adjustments to your trades to benefit more.

Example

Take the example where you invest in ABC stock at a price of $53 per share. You invest in this particular stock in the hope that the price will rise albeit modestly. At the same time, you wish to sell a 60-day covered call of ABC stock at a price of $55 per share. However, within a few days, you get to find out through a news item that ABC stock has good prospects in the long term.

This information changes your outlook so that you are now of the opinion that the stock price could actually rise to about $70 per share within six months. This catches your interest because your initial estimate about the profitability of ABC stock has increased exponentially. In such circumstances, there are a couple of things that you could do.

This is a clear demonstration of how a covered call with set positions and initial forecasts can go through some changes. It also could be that the initial forecast was wrong. As such, you have some options, and you can take action. Rolling action can help you switch your strategy and have a different approach.

Now if the stock price increases and you have no intention of selling the stock, then you will need better management skills as well as high assignment risks simply because the covered call that you have is now in the money. As such, you choose to purchase all your covered calls in order to cancel out any obligation to sell the stock. It is advisable at this stage to then sell a call option that has little chance of being assigned at a better strike price.

The common strategy when a stock forecast or objective changes is to adopt a rolling process. Rolling covered calls are usually adapted by seasoned traders. Even then, as a trader, you should understand that there is really no specific formula about the implementation of a rolling plan. For instance, as a trader, you may be wondering the current covered call should be shut down and replaced with yet another call that is in line with the new changes. If the answer is yes, will you prefer a covered call with a further expiration date and higher strike price compared to the previous call? There is generally not a correct or wrong solution and what you think is the best approach, should do. This is why experts say that covered call rolling is a decision that is subjective, and all investors and traders should take it into consideration in an individual and careful manner.

Rolling up a covered call

The process of rolling up a strategy like a covered call, for instance, entails buying out a position as well as closing existing covered call options. At the same time, you will sell a covered call with a higher strike price but similar expiration dates and the same underlying stock.

Rolling example

Our previous situation had the stock ABC at a price per share of $79. In this instance, the trader thinks the stock will trade within a confined range in the coming two months. As such, the trader decides to create a covered position by selling 1 ABC Call at $80 and then this price suddenly moves to $83 so that the call option is now at $85. While there are costs involved in making the adjustments, the possible benefits are much higher in essence.

Initial covered call: ABC stock costs $79 and has an expiration period of 60 days till October. The first step in this instance is to create another covered call by purchasing ABC shares at a price of $79. The next step would be to sell ABC stock at $80 with each call selling at a price of $2.50.

2. How to Roll the Short Strangle

Rolling is the process of making adjustments to options strategies that a trader sets up. There are varied reasons why traders actually make adjustments to their trades. These include erroneous initial predictions, changing market positions, and news that will affect the performance of a stock.

Now on a strangle strategy you always have a negative delta on the put and a positive delta on the call option. Therefore, we can deduce that we have a neutral delta in this instance. A neutral delta is okay at the onset. However, if the position remains that way then you lose money. As a trader, your desire is to make money; therefore, when there is movement in the stock price you want this movement to be huge. As such you may use gamma which will ensure the price goes up. However, should the stock price remain constant without any movement then you will lose money.

The short strangle is sometimes considered by traders as a very risky strategy. However, as an experienced trader who knows what he is doing; this is not necessarily the case. Here is a look at some circumstances where risk is reduced by rolling action.

First of all, premium is considered rather rich. As it is, a short straddle requires a trader to sell a put option, and a call option based on an underlying option with similar expiration dates and strike price. The best ones are the ones that offer a very rich premium under near-the-money or at-the-money conditions.

Also, it is crucial that short straddles have expiration dates that are within one month or less. It is time decay that causes the value of options to decline. This is why short straddles should be limited to only short-term options. Time decay often happens extremely fast within the first month.

Traders should focus their eyes on the current price, and the strike price then note the relationship. It is advisable to close positions once it becomes practically possible. This should happen especially when positions begin to move in the money. It is always a great idea to close at a profit because time decay will affect the value of the trade.

Also, keep a lookout for time decay. Therefore, once it begins to occur, you should plan to close the positions entered. Also, it is advisable to consider duplicating the strategy should the intrinsic value advance too fast. The forward movement in some instance can be unavoidable depending on certain factors such as price movement direction. In short, the price of the stock will not be volatile and as such time decay could have a positive effect on the two sides.

3. Rolling a Short Call Spread

When you roll a spread, the action is similar to rolling a single option. A trader who rolls a short call spread is most probably exit a position in a timely fashion with the strike prices moving down or up. The difference between rolling the short call spread and an individual option is that with the short call spread you will be engaged in a four-way trade. You will essentially be trading four different options instead of the usual two. This means opening two new positions while closing two existing ones.

Example

Let's say you have ABC stock that is trading at a price of $53. After a while, you begin to have bearish thoughts about this stock believing that the price will eventually go down. As such, you choose to sell a 30-day short call spread at 55/60. For this, you receive $1 per contract.

After some time, you realize that your prediction was wrong, and the price of ABC stock was not going to go down. The stock, instead of acting bearish suddenly turns bullish. ABC stock suddenly moves from the initial price of $53 to a short-term price of $55. At this juncture, your short call spread still has 15 days left to expiration. If you are to buy back the option, it would cost you $1.80 per contract. In this instance, you may choose to believe your initial forecast or follow the current trend.

If you choose to follow your initial analysis, then you may need to roll the strategy. When you do so, you will roll the expiration time out further and increase the strike price. As such, you will need to buy back at $1.80 the call spreads you sold at $1. You will then sell a short call spread with 45 days till expiration, a long strike price of $65 and a shirt strike price of $60. You will sell these options are a price of $1.10 per contract.

At the start of this position, you were $0.80 down because of selling the options $1 and buying at $1.80. However, after the rolling process, should the ABC stock price be below $60 at the prevailing expiration date, then you will be ahead with the $0.30. You should hope that all your analysis was correct and that this stock will expire below the $60 mark. This way, you will end the trade at a profit. However, should this not happen, then you will begin incurring losses pretty fast.

Basically, if you implement a roll process on a stock option position, be careful not to compound your losses because this is something that is quite possible. Therefore, if you are confident about your initial predictions, you should try and stick to your game plan. Alternatively, you could choose to exit the strategy rather than roll and incur even larger losses.

This particular roll management process applies to most two-legged trades and not just the short spreads. Rolling also applies to other formations including back spreads and straddles.

4. Rolling Short Put Spreads – cash secured

Let us use an example to understand how this roll operation works. Let us assume that you have sold a cash-secured put option with underlying stock ABC at a strike price of $50. During the process, you sold some put options and received $0.9 per contract even as ABC price at the time was $51. After some time, the price of ABC stock dropped to $48.5 as it approaches expiration.

Some of the few options that you have as a trader include purchasing back some of the options that you sold. As such you will buy back options with the strike price of $50 before these are reassigned. The major challenge now is that you will buy back the options at a price of $1.55 even though you purchased the same at a price of $0.90.

There are several tools that you can use when rolling the call. One of these is making use of Ally Invest spread order screen. When you use this screen, you will notice that you can actually buy the $50 strike price option. As you execute this trade, you will also sell options with a $47.50 price which is an actual roll down of the strategy. This will have a 90-day expiration period, and the cost per trade is $1.70. As such, you will receive a net credit of $15 for 100 share contracts at $0.15.

The example above indicates clearly how you can roll out and actually save yourself from an impending loss or improve an existing position. There will also be a significant increase in the time value which is crucial after obtaining the 90-day option.

Let us assume that put with the $47.50 strike price goes on to expire worthless after a period of 90 days then you will gain $1.05 per each. This will eventually earn you $105 per contract. Even then, you need to take precaution because you could be taking a loss every time you roll down. Also, you should secure any gains that you make in the market. When you do not, then you risk compounding your losses. This kind of risk is not worth it so always take precaution when rolling out positions.

Always make sure that you roll out within the shortest time so as to face fewer risks in the market. Sometimes it may be necessary to incur some costs in order to roll out a position. Once a position than you have sold gets into the money, you will need to make a determination as to whether rolling is necessary. Basically, you need to think about rolling a position before it gains more than 2% to 4% in the money. This will also be based on other factors such as market conditions, volatility, and value of the stocks among others.

If you let a position get too much into the money, it will be difficult to end up in a profitable position. Also, think about what is known as a preemptive roll which basically dictates that you should implement any rollouts on positions before options get into the money. Do so if you think the position is headed that way. This lowers your rolling costs and makes it much better for you as a trader.

5. Rolling out a Butterfly Position

As a trader, you need to have a great trading plan that allows adjustments to positions that you have taken in the market. This is because markets and positions keep changing in the course of a trading period. Therefore it is advisable to work within a set of guidelines rather than a set of strict rules.

Butterfly trade example

Take the example of the ABC April 2016 put options butterfly strategy that was set up with a long call. The long call is initiated for hedging the upside of the trade. An unforeseen instance happened where the price of ABC stock went up steeply while the trade did not have a promising outlook.

After about a week's time, some adjustments became necessary. In our case above, the most appropriate solution was to initiate a rolling process. To do this effectively, it was determined that another butterfly position with a long call should be introduced. The initial butterfly is therefore rolled so that its outlook improves to avoid incurring unnecessary losses.

Making the adjustment is crucial because it helped save an otherwise desperation situation. As it is, such adjustments serve numerous purposes, but the best are those that allow trades to proceed to a conclusion and within desirable profit margins.

It is essential to note that the intervention described above as one that was not based on any rules and had not been initially planned. It was only designed and executed when the need arose and based on the needs at the time. This is basically how trades are supposed to be executed as well as intervention methods such as rolling. You will find that this kind of approach works best and helps to reduce risks and improve outlooks.

6. Adjusting a Butterfly to a Condor

As a trader, you may set up a butterfly position which may then experience certain challenges that may cost you significant losses. One of the options you may want to consider is turning the position from a butterfly to a condor.

A butterfly spread can easily be split into two distinct spreads.

Ideally, you will want to split the original butterfly and create an additional butterfly. When you do this, you will come up with a condor. You will still have two spreads but with completely different sold strikes. At this juncture, you would not necessarily adjust the butterfly. However, the intervention is necessary especially when the price of the underlying stock was rising and while other indicators showed the option was headed towards a loss.

Making such adjustments is necessary especially where losses seem inevitable based on conditions, but the situation can be rescued. But the interventions should be designed and implemented based on market trends, conditions, volatility, price action, and other related factors.

Chapter 2: Strategic Planning for Options Trading

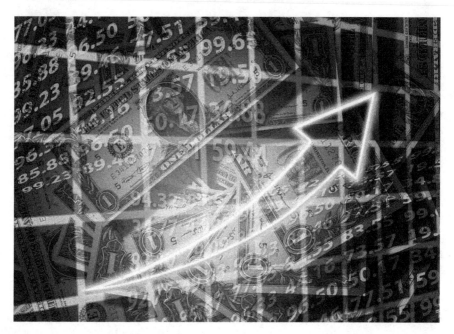

Strategic planning is an integral part of sustainable success, be it in business or in options trading. Let's talk about how to make a game plan for your trades in this chapter.

What is Strategic Planning

For starting a business, you need a blueprint, a plan. Without any direction or planning, nothing works. Options are the same way. To make great trades consistently, you need a solid strategic plan. On top of all this, options aren't simply buying something cheap and selling it at a higher price to make a profit. It's infinitely more complex than that. There are basically two types of options namely the call options and the put options, but they're simultaneously two kinds of strategies too. You purchase in one and sell in the other. It all depends on your inclination towards being bearish or bullish. But options wouldn't be complicated at all if there were just these two strategies.

Earlier in this book, it has been mentioned, that there are a lot of complex mathematical operations that have to be done to calculate and formulate a plethora of strategies. The basic ingredients of all these strategies are the two primary options namely the call and put options. The multitudes of strategies that are so formulated are the different permutations and combinations of these two and other things.

CBOE- Chicago Board of Options Exchange is the largest such exchange in the world, which offers options on a wide variety of single stocks, indexes, and ETFs. Traders can create multiple option strategies varying from buying or selling a single option to very complex and intricate ones that include multiple simultaneous option positions.

Benefits it Offers

To prevent your emotions from affecting the trade, a plan needs to be created. Experiencing the otherworldly happiness of making a huge gain or a heartbreaking amount of loss can make your mind spin, and you might deviate from the original strategy you had in mind if you had one, which you need to. Strategic planning helps you with that. It gives you detailed yet simplified instructions on specifically how to tackle every trading situation, should they arise. If you are following a well-formed strategy efficiently, you can even handle multiple trades. Thus, you don't need to skip a good opportunity if presented with it. However, taking up too many trades may expose you to too much risk. A well-structured trading strategy tells you both how you are making trades and the reason for which you're doing it.

Not only has that, but good strategic planning also guided you on how to monitor the results. One should know whether the strategy they're applying is working in the desired manner. Random trades where one just sells and buys for any reason which seems good, does not give any useful feedback, because the gains and losses will be as random as the impulses which made the trade. But by using strategic planning, the right amount calibrated adjustments can be made to the trading process to improve it overall.

It allows you to be proactive

When you have a plan, you can predict the future better and prepare accordingly. It helps you anticipate unfavorable scenarios and take the necessary actions to avoid negative impacts. This way, you are not just reacting to negative situations but are rather proactively avoiding them. Market trends are ever-changing, and if you want to stay on top of your game, you need always to be proactive to stay ahead of the competition.

It gives you a sense of direction

With a strategic plan, you get a bearing of where you currently stand and in what direction you need to go in order to achieve your goals and objectives. When your plan is in sync with your vision and goals, you go forward with that much energy. It also helps you make more efficient decisions and evaluate your success better.

Tips to Develop a Strategic Plan

Now that we've established the need for a strategic plan, we need to know about certain things to develop a strategic plan. Developing a strategic plan takes into consideration a lot of factors.

- **The amount of capital you have**

- **The type of capital you have**

- **Your inclination towards being a bull or a bear**

- **The existing conditions in the market**

- **Market volatility**

- **Technical environment**

- **Your affinity with risk**

- **Are you a long term or short-term investor?**

- **Your technical knowledge and expertise**

Now, this list is not exhaustive but covers a major chunk of all the things you need to take into consideration while developing a strategic plan. Coming to the tips to develop a strategic plan, just know that options are not like any other investments. They require deep analysis and detailed, methodical approaches. So, the first tip would be to see how much capital you have and then choose a strategic plan, which will work efficiently with the amount of capital you have. If you do not have a lot of capital, start with a short-term strategy, which generates profits early so you can gather some more capital and prepare yourself for a more intensive investment. However, with more profit potential comes more risk, and that's where your risk preference comes in. If you're a safe player who wants a stable income even though the rate is lower, then plan a strategy that gives you low but regular returns. If you're a risk taker, then you can aim for greater profits, but take note that you should ideally not invest in higher risk strategies with borrowed capital because the overall liability might increase. Invest in such strategies with your own money and profits, which do not have any inherent liabilities. Another tip would be to determine the direction you want to go with, whether it's going to be a bearish approach or bullish approach. But at the same time, another auxiliary tip would be, to be flexible with your approach. If your general trading style is inclined to the bearish side, but it's reasonably apparent that being a bull about now would be better, and vice versa, then being rigid is not good.

Chapter 3: Understanding the Greeks

When you think of the word "Greeks," the mighty Olympians may come to your mind, but we're studying options, aren't we? Now that we know what options are, it's time to move on to the options strategies. But is it? Before we do that, it is important to understand what the Greeks are and their relevance in affecting the price of every option you'll trade in. The examples being used here are hypothetical in nature and don't represent real-world scenarios.

An investment has a lot of risks, and through options, one can manage these risks. Minimal risk strategies are opted by conventional investors but to earn more profits, a lot of investors go for bolder strategies that involve more risk. And the thing about options is, one can measure and modify the risk of any stock market investment.

It is when you calculate the different risks, that a set of Greek letters, the group of which is known as 'The Greeks' are put in use to measure or express in certain quantifiable terms, the risks which one faces in an investment.

Now I know you might be wondering what Vega is doing here since it's not a Greek letter. Don't worry about that; it's inconsequential. What our real focus should be on is that by using the Greeks of a position, certain risk variables are measured and can be modified to bear the risk endurance of the investor. Let's start the introduction.

The relevance of The Gamma

Gamma is important because it has a direct effect on the one Greek that greatly determines the value of stock options most, which is the Delta. We know how delta changes now. But what is the quantity by which options Delta changes? Think of the Gamma as velocity. While speed is a scalar quantity, which measures only the magnitude, Gamma is the vector quantity, which means it measures the magnitude and the direction of the change.

The significance of Gamma is for directional and hedging trades.

- For Directional trades, to get an overall position, gamma needs to incline towards the direction of interest, so that option delta increases with the development of trade.

- For hedging trades, you would need as low gamma as possible on overall options to make sure the options trading position remains very neutral to changes in the underlying stock.

Options Gamma does not matter much when one is buying a call or put options for one a directional trade as one can be sure that they're already purchasing positive options gamma meaning that delta of your options will rise with a rise or fall in the stock.

Theta

Thus, we can say that Theta measures the everyday percentage of depreciation of a stock option's price with the underlying stock showing no change. It represents the rate of time decay of options.

It is directly proportional to the Gamma, which means more the gamma, more the theta. While an option is having high gamma return very high profits with stock price changes, but it has a higher theta too, which impairs the price of the option quickly.

But in case, no significant movement happens early, the option could lose substantial money. So, with an aggressive option position, you should also consider the high risk associated because of the higher options theta. The tradeoff needs to be favorable.

The theta is lower for OTM options than it is for ATM options because the dollar amount of time value is smaller.

Vega

A stock option has two main components related to price.

1. Intrinsic value

2. Extrinsic value

Vega does not affect the intrinsic value but affects the time value of an option's price. Thus, the longer-term options will have a higher Vega than shorter-term options.

Step-by-step Entry Guide

Before you start making any trades, there are certain things you should check. This is a strategic step-by-step guide that will help you pick great trades and filter out bad trades consistently. The order facilitates quickly figuring out whether a trade is worth your time.

Portfolio Balance

Portfolio balance is everything. So even before you begin looking for a new trade, you need to ask yourself how it will fit in your portfolio. You need to question whether you need the trade. If, for example, you already have a lot of bullish trades in your portfolio, you probably don't need another one.

Balancing out trades is the key to developing a good portfolio as it reduces risk. So, when you already have a handful of bullish trades, you should be looking for some bearish trades that will offset your risk. When you know what kind of trade you need to look for from the get-go, it helps you filter better and focus only on what your portfolio needs.

Liquidity

Liquidity is one of the most important factors when it comes to picking great, tradable stocks. An illiquid option is not worth your time. So, when looking for a new trade, you should follow this general rule of thumb: if the underlying stock trades approximately 100k shares daily, then it's good to go. Since it's a big and efficient market, we can be confident in the fact that the calculations will only become more accurate as time passes. For underlying options, if the strikes you are trading have at least 1000 open interest contracts, this is preferable. This makes sure you can get in and out of the market fast as it is liquid enough.

Implied Volatility Percentile

Once we've picked out the trades that pass the previous two criteria, the next step is to check whether the IV is relatively low or high. This is measured using IV percentiles. So, for example, if GOOG has IV of 40% but an IV percentile of 80%, this means that over the last year, more than 80% of the time the volatility would be lower than it currently is (40%). This implies that the implied volatility for GOOG is relatively high, meaning you should consider premium-selling strategies.

Similarly, if FB has an IV of 35% but an IV percentile of 30%, it means that over the last year, only 30% of the time the IV was lower than what it is currently (35%). This also implies that there is a 70% chance the IV will increase, so the IV is relatively low for FB and you should prefer to be a net buyer.

Picking a Strategy

When we talk about picking the best strategy, it is more about eliminating than selecting. Once you have a good grasp of how the underlying stock's IV and IV percentile affect the options, you can start eliminating strategies that wouldn't make sense here. For example, in case the option pricing is rich, and IV is high, we can eliminate strategies like calendars, long single options, debit spreads, etc. Then we can go ahead and select the best strategy from the ones left (credit spreads, strangles, iron condors, etc.) depending on our account size and risk tolerance.

Strikes & Month

Once you have selected the right strategy, the next step is to place trades at a probability level you're comfortable with. Say, you're going to be selling credit spreads below the market. You could sell your credit spreads at a strike price that gives you a 70% chance of success or a strike price that gives you a 90% chance of success. Both are high probability trades, but one is clearly more aggressive. You can pick either one if you're sure it fits your goals and your style. You also need to give yourself enough time to make sure the trade can work for you. For high IV strategies, you'd want to place them at 30-60 days out, and for low IV strategies, you'd want to go with 60-90 days. Why? Because the longer timeline boosts your theta value and counters the low volatility.

Position Size

One of the most crucial areas where many traders - even the experienced ones - fail is position sizing. Once you've gone through all the previous steps, you should carefully evaluate your position size before placing a trade. There have been numerous studies that have shown that your risk increases exponentially when trading big positions, and you could easily end up blowing up your whole account. This is why for beginners and intermediates I advise going with a small position at all times. Place all your trades on a sliding scale of 1-5% of your total balance. This is your risk scale.

How do you define risk? Simple, it's the cash or margin you put up to cover a trade. If you were to sell a $1 wide credit put spread for 25 cents, you would need to put up $75 margin to cover it. Now, if your account is worth $10,000, and for each trade, you wish to allocate 2% of your account, the $75 margin is what would be used to base the trade-off. So, you can take $200 of risk (2% of $10,000) divided by $75 per contract. This comes out at 2.66, which means you could sell 2.66 spreads at most.

To be safe, you should always round it down, never up.

Future Moves

Just like chess players need to be thinking a few moves ahead (at least the good ones do), a good trader also needs to be thinking ahead. You should always have a Plan B for when things go wrong, and this should mean more than just being able to shield yourself from a losing trade.

Although that is important, you should also be thinking about scenarios where the stock doesn't move, and you might have to roll it over to the next month. You need to know whether the options even exist for the next contract month. The stock might have earnings coming up soon, or a dividend might be paid out soon.

You need to remember that some trades **will** go wrong, as is the way of the market. If you're constantly asking yourself important questions, your brain stays alert and formulates new plans to adjust if the need arises.

Fundamentals of Options Strategies

Long calls

It is the simplest option strategy to learn about. That does not mean the profit-making is easy. It is a bullish strategy, but one must be right about many things to make it profitable. For that, a trader needs to be right about the direction of the stock price movement and the quantum of it. The time it takes to move must also be correct. Right on all these three elements makes the long call strategy profitable. The upside profit potential is unlimited but things like volatility and time erosion work against a long option.

Short Calls

These are not good for newbies in options trading. It is also called a naked call, as it is uncovered. It is quite a risky position because the upside risk here is unlimited and the profit is limited (happens when the stock price drops). Short Call Write is a credit strategy where you get money for putting on the position, which puts the broker at risk if you are not able to cover the position when required.

Long puts

Like a long call trade, a long-put trade is simple to understand. Put strategies are generally harder to make a profit in, but the strategy is a basic component of many complex options strategies. A long-put option is bearish in terms of inclination. With long calls, an investor needs to be right about the direction of stock price movement and the amount of it with the time frame to make a profit. The maximum potential loss on a long-put trade equals the price paid for the option. The profit potential, however, is quite substantial if the stock price drops.

Short puts

The short puts are not as risky as the short calls. But that in no way means that newbies in option trading can easily make profits using this strategy. When a put is sold, a profit/loss situation opposite to that of a long put is created. The profit, when the stock price rises, is limited to the premium received on selling the option. The downside risk keeps rising until the stock's value is zero. The margin requirements of this strategy are high, and thus, significant funds are required.

Selecting your strike price

Options traders often have a hard time determining the strike prices they are going to use. The type of strike price (ATM, OTM, and ITM) affects the quantum of the movement of the underlying asset price required to make a profit. Even if the underlying stock remains stagnant, profit can be made by using an appropriate strike price. The bearishness or the bullishness of the investor needs to be matched accordingly.

Bullish options strategies

If an investor is extremely bearish, out of the money long puts or in-the-money short calls should be considered. These require a highly bearish move of an equally high quantum in the underlying stock to become profitable. But if you're not that bearish, ITM long puts or OOTM short calls should be considered. OOTM can result in a profit sometimes, even when there's no price change in the underlying stock.

Bearish options strategies

Most option strategies have a higher profit potential when they need a substantial price movement in the underlying stock, but it's also less likely to make a profit. OOTM short puts and OOTM short calls can make a profit possible even with zero movement in the underlying stock. But they are extremely risky. Using credit spreads is a safer alternative but has less profit potential.

Chapter 4: Choosing a Brokerage Account

When selecting an online broker for your options trading, there's one essential principle- There is no replacement for options experience. Obviously, make your own decisions. Because somebody loves a broker does not mean you will— or that you need to utilize them.

What you need to do, in any case, is build up a plan for assessing the brokers you consider, so you will guarantee that the one you eventually pick offers the features you need—and certainly require.

The Importance of Choosing the Right Broker

Not all firms will have the capacity to give the affirmations you need regarding all your worries. The more things you need to consider with respect to the "mechanics" of online trading, the more opportunities will be made available for you to end up diverted and falter as you move along the way to options trading.

In case you are a genuinely new trader, you may likewise need to check whether the broker offers any close to home, one-on-one investment counsel, or proposes trading chances to customers. Relatively few online firms do, yet in the event that such things are important to you, it does not hurt to inquire. You may, at any rate, get a referral to a partnered warning service or data site that can help give some trading thoughts.

This enables a client to manage a prepared options broker to deal with orders and questions. The commission charges are not quite the same as the online rates—yet the value offered by having a live broker will most likely be worth the expense in case you are simply taking in the trading ropes.

Obviously, the essence of online trading is accomplishing direct access to the trades, so you can perform your transactions precisely like the experts. In this way, you should attempt to wean yourself from the requirement for broker help before going online—or as fast as possible from there on.

Important Broker Qualities

Choosing a good broker is crucial in order to make sure all parts of your plan are implemented. A big mistake that many traders make is not finding a broker. This doesn't always mean going to some guy's office, so he can tell you exactly what to do. There are online brokers that don't tell you what to do in any form. The decisions are left up to you and you have the tools to make your own choices.

The biggest reason that traders don't want to get a broker is because they aren't free. Some require a payment up front, and most will take a commission fee, meaning you won't always make as much from your returns. Not everyone that trades has a broker, but for a beginner, it's important to get some help from one. Even if you manage to go through your first few months without needing much of their advice, it's still an insurance policy that can give you peace of mind. While you might have to pay out a fee, it's much better to give that money than to end up losing it all anyway.

The Standard of the Trading Software

For online traders, this is the most basic issue, and it takes various inquiries to decide exactly what number of features is incorporated—and how great they are. Is the software user-friendly; easy to comprehend and simple to utilize? Can I get it on a disk or would I be able to download it from the internet? Is it hard to install on my PC? Will I require help?

If you don't have access to such resources, you should check if it requires any unique equipment or communications highlights, for example, high-speed modems, specialty internet browsers or DSL lines—with the end goal to make it work proficiently. Check if it incorporates adequate pricing and logical, analytical tools for your requirements.

If it does not include these things, check if it is built to be effortlessly incorporated into independent quotation frameworks and analytical services. Is satisfactory customer documentation given—both printed and online—to enable both to understand the framework and manage any technical issues?

Another question to ask about the standard of the trading software is whether it is attractive to look at—and, in the event that you do not like it, would you be able to change such things as size or color or display? This may appear to be unimportant, yet in case you will be an active trader, you might take a look at it on and off for six or seven hours every day. Thus, you need to ensure that it is something that you do not end up hating.

Simplicity of Order Entry and Transmission Speed

The simplicity of order entry and transmission speed is additionally critical for active traders, who might put in heaps of requests and need the procedure to be as programmed as possible. Ask yourself: What number of fields on the order-entry screen do I need to fill in to put in a request? Determine if you need to type in all the data, or if the software imports it from the logical or pricing screens in the event that you need it to.

Do I need to manually go back to the firm's order screen, or would I be able to get to it by tapping on the screens given by incorporated trading partners? Does the program send the order to the trade when I submit it, or does it need to be prepared elsewhere inside the firm first? Do I need to indicate the trade where the order is sent, or does the program shop around at the best cost and course the order as need be?

You will want to determine if you have to put orders specifically through the software, or if you have a browser to get to your framework. Figure out if orders need to be entered at night-time, for execution the next day—or just while the market is open. Consider if you can also put orders from the site and also through the software.

Quality of Service

The quality of service is one important factor in determining if a brokerage is right for you. Start by asking: Are there independent order screens for stocks and options? If not, can the order screen be personalized to take into account options traders? Are the options quotes given in the order screen constantly or deferred?

In the event that you call up an option chain, determine if it is a real-time preview, or a delayed collation of last prices. Furthermore, explore if it is spread out in an orderly way, or if you must search for the option you need. Does the option-pricing framework give you access to current bids and offers, or simply last trading prices? What about volume numbers? Open interest?

Determine if the framework includes multi-option strategies, for example, spreads, and give you a chance to order them as a unit. If so, make sure it charges one commission for such orders—or survey fees for every option in the combination. Ask if the framework will settle for stop and stop-limit orders on options.

What about stops and buy orders that are dependent upon the price of the basic asset? Do any of the incorporated quote services specialize in options? If yes, will their program give me a chance to punch in trade parameters and screen for good trading chances? Does the brokerage firm's program have any comparable services to assist me with options analysis?

Timely Executions and Confirmations

The broker's order entry program ought to give guided access to the electronic trading frameworks of the suitable trades, and, once your trades qualify for programmed execution, report back a confirmation in few seconds— ideally to an area of the order-entry screen where you can quickly observe that you got your fill. In the event that the trade does not qualify the bill for programmed execution, it ought to show up in a corner on your screen intended to give you a chance to monitor your working orders.

Framework Capacity

The broker's database ought to have the adequate reserve processing capacity to deal with additional overwhelming order stream—and the firm ought to have a framework set up to manage quick economic situations as successfully as possible. (No firm is flawless when such circumstances occur, yet they should strive to make an attempt to at the very least—not simply hurl their hands and say, "Sorry" or "Too bad!")

Commission Costs

Numerous traders would put commissions much higher on the list than other important quality factors; however, our reasoning is unique. What great are low commissions in the event that you get lousy prices, moderate executions and terrible (or no) benefit? Ensure the broker gives you all that you need—and require—and do not stress on the chance that it cost a couple of additional dollars.

You will likely influence it up on your trades, at any rate. Do, in any case, demand that the broker's fees, at any rate, be competitive; you need to pay for what you get—not pay to get gouged. Additionally, make sure to get some information about possibly precarious things covered up underneath a guarantee of low commissions—e.g., a commission rate of $1 per option would not help you a whole lot if the firm forces a $50 least on each order.

Customer Support

Very important! It's a must have—ideally by telephone, not only online, by email or through a self-improvement menu on the site (in spite of the fact that it's pleasant to have those choices too). Likewise, see if support is accessible simply amid business hours — or terribly, just when the market's open. Your goal is to guarantee that the help services will be accessible on the occasions you really require help.

Order Execution Backups

There might be times when things turn out badly—even with the best broker and the most superb programming. In the event that it occurs within trading hours, your broker must have a backup framework to manage it. That implies having enough telephone lines and in-house individuals to deal with client calls and the sudden flood of disconnected order stream.

All things considered, no trader who frantically needs to escape a position 30 minutes before the end wants to call his broker and hear a tinny, computer voice, "All agents are presently occupied; however, your call is vital to us. Please stay on the line; a delegate will be with you in roughly 45 minutes"— soon after you have lost your shirt!

Security of Individual and Financial Data

Numerous individuals fear to do anything online in light of the fact that they fear a hacker, or another person will discover about them, take their identity—or, more terribly, take their money. In substantial part, these fears are unreasonable—particularly inside the frameworks of America's financial services systems, which were planned in view of security and had unique assurances, set up. Therefore, most brokerage frameworks are as secure as it's presently conceivable to make them. All things considered, it never hurts to make an inquiry.

Best Brokers Specifically for Options Trading

Not all brokers operate in the same manner, so it's important to make sure you are finding one that will work with your methods of option trading. Some brokers specialize in penny stocks while others strictly work with options. While you might know someone that personally deals with a specific type, make sure you are still using a broker that has an extensive comprehension of options so that you can implement the best strategies.

The biggest flaw in any trader is inexperience. You might make the wrong investments here and there, or lose money that you could have expanded, but the main reason for this in the end is usually inexperience. If you are investing in a person that's specifically to combat this big mistake, you want to make sure they have a track record that proves their relevancy.

E-Trade's

Options House platform and mobile application are the highest quality levels of option trading platforms. Options House at present gives traders premium-quality tools without the top-notch price tag.

TD Ameritrade

This online broker compensates for higher-than-normal trading commissions with superior service, research, and trading tools that will make everybody from amateur investors to active traders upbeat. **This one** is best for beginners and has the best options tools.

Interactive Brokers

Interactive Brokers is a solid option for cutting edge, frequent traders. The broker offers worldwide trade abilities, low commissions, and a quality trading platform. Be careful though, because new traders may be killed by inertia fees, high parity necessities and an absence of instructive assets.

Charles Schwab

Charles Schwab has earned its solid reputation. The broker offers top-notch client benefits, two powerful trading platforms and a wide range of commission-free ETFs and no-transaction-fee shared assets. **This option** is best for order types.

Ally

Ally is a vigorous trading platform and a line-up of free research, outlining, information and logical devices make it a decent decision for active traders. But on the other hand, it's proper for starting investors who will value that there is no minimum for the account and no yearly fees. This one is the best low-cost broker and can be **found here**.

Trade Station

Trade Station is the best quality website for trading active stock, futures and options. This brokerage is for investors who depend on the broker's high-octane trading platform, reams of research, and modern logical tools. The firm gives three commission plans including flat fee, per contract/per share and unbundled pricing plan. The absence of commission-free ETFs and common assets can be a turnoff to few investors. Overall, it's a well-rounded offering

Fidelity

Fidelity is a platform that shows traders the correct way to do things and gives them every resource they require as the trading goes. Options trading can be scary and confounding for new traders. Fidelity offers a huge collection of free research and information introduced in a way that is not overpowering for inexperienced traders. **This** is the best option for research and training.

Tasty works

Tasty works has become famous in options trading. The brokerage, driven by its parent financial media organization, Tasty Trade, offers probably the best rates in options trading matched with incredible tools and options for traders.

E Options

E Options gives a proficient, nitty-gritty platform for active investors who prefer low expenses to an extravagant platform. The investment funds can be critical for cutting-edge stock and options traders who have different sources for the research and information they require.

Creating a Backup Plan

Be absolutely mindful, nonetheless, that regardless of how good a brokerage firm is being painted, you will more than likely run into an issue or two while preceding before all is said and done. These could be the consequence of disturbances at the exchanges, with your broker's database, or with your own computer, internet connection, or telephone line.

You could even commit an exorbitant error as the consequence of stupid calculation errors. Approximately fourteen years back, we signed onto our internet browser to check the news and opening market indices —and nearly hopped into frenzy mode when the EarthLink™ start page showed the Dow down 397.85 for just 10 minutes after the opening.

Obviously, it was simply a terrible calculation error; the Dow was down simply 7.85—however, the browser's numbers were not right throughout the day. Had we followed up on those numbers, it could have been a catastrophe. Be that as it may, that is only the manner in which it is in today's powered-up world, kept running by PCs, encouraged by telephone lines and absolutely subject to the ideal execution of electrical transmission lines.

To shield yourself from the impacts of these mechanical caprices, build up a reinforcement plan that goes past simply hoping to get the telephone and call your broker when the framework goes down. Create a plan in which you are certain you generally have both limits as well as stops set up on your weak positions—both profitable and unprofitable.

Be certain you completely comprehend the risks before attempting new strategies or starting new plays. Print out day by day copies of your open positions in the event that the broker's server fails. Closely observing your account status, particularly your equity balance, and print hard copies of key account outlines at any rate week by week.

With those protections set up, technical issues may cost you a little loss. However, you will never confront an overwhelming financial difficulty. What's more, should the broker encounter a total framework disappointment, your paper duplicates will kill any plausibility of debate in regard to your positions and value of accounts.

These concerns are legitimate. However, they are not really motivations to shy away from options trading— particularly given the technological and innovative advancements.

Remaining Cautious with Brokers

One last admonition about picking a broker: Just because a sales representative or promotional material says a brokerage firm offers some new feature on their software or an exceptional service does not imply that it's quite true. As we know, some marketers are emissaries of frivolity, preferring to promote the positive and disregard the negative. In this manner, the cases you read delivered by the firms themselves might be painfully exaggerated.

In all truth, managers and programmers frequently tell advertisement marketing specialists that some new service or product highlight will be available when the promotion turns out, and then fail to meet their own schedule. What's more, sales representatives are every now and then told things that are non-existent work better than they do— and, not being experts and ready to decide for themselves, just pass the misrepresentations along.

Try to do more other than converse with the brokerage agent. Look at some reviews, online and in popular financial magazines, here and there. Then speak with people who have been in the industry for a very long time.

Chapter 5: Making Short-term Trading Work

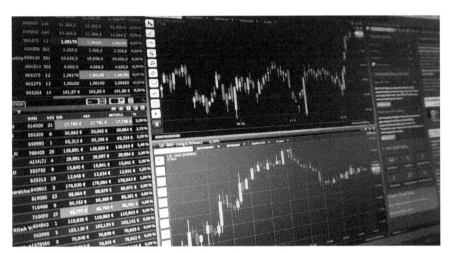

Short-term options trading is an excellent pursuit for beginner options traders, but also, and perhaps surprisingly, for more experienced and seasoned options traders as well. In fact, short-term options are becoming more popular within the options world. "Weekly" options, in particular, have undergone a rather rapid growth in popularity in recent years, and seem to bring a substantial amount of success to those who decide to utilize them. For those still unsure about what a weekly option entails, it's essentially just an option that expires in one week. Typically, an asset is posted on Thursday, and expires that following Friday.

But aside from that, short-term options are also excellent trading pursuits because they decrease the financial risk associated with options. With short-term options trading, trades are handled relatively quickly, which means you don't need to commit months or years of your time to an asset that may or may not generate meaningful profit. So, short-term options trading means, generally speaking, less risks, less waiting time, and quicker gain opportunities. Sounds pretty great, right?

Fortunately, short-term trading is something both beginner and experienced options traders can take advantage of. The short-term trading strategies that you employ will of course depend upon your level and experience, and so, because this book is geared toward beginner options traders seeking to generate profit in just 48 hours, we'll be discussing several short-term trading strategies and suggestions in particular. These are foundational strategies that are easy to understand, and even easier to use. Sure, they're not the fanciest, nor are they the most impressive, but they won't require over excessive risks and won't put your financial status on the line.

Because this book revolves around helping you trade options successfully in just 48 hours, I'd recommend the following:

- Dedicate Day-1 of trading to understanding, practicing, and employing the first short-term strategy that we're going to discuss shortly—married put.

- Dedicate Day-2 of trading to understanding, practicing, and utilizing the second short-term strategy that we're going to discuss after married put—straddling. Married Put

Married puts are one of the basic, but surprisingly helpful, short-term trading strategies currently available to both new and experienced traders. Essentially, a married put, sometimes called a protective put, is when an investor buys shares of a stock, while simultaneously buying put options for those same purchased stocks. To break this concept down even further, consider this:

- John the options trader invests in stock A, B, and C.

- When he invests in stock A, B, and C, he also purchases put options for stock A, B, and C.

At this point you should understand why the married put strategy is an excellent choice—it's clear, simple, and reliable protection for your investments. But here's the best part: married puts, technically, create unlimited profit generation potential, and eliminate potential loss caused from downwards stock growth.

Straddling

The short-term options trading strategy of straddling can be, for some, a bit more complicated than married put. This isn't to say, however, that it's not an equally reliable and successful strategy for beginner traders to employ. With the straddling technique, investors will buy both a put and call option for the same stock, with the same strike price, and with the same expiration date.

Now, to fully understand how this strategy works, you'll need to be familiar with:

1. Put options

2. Call options

3. Strike price

Chapter 1's discussion about options types will help clarify any questions you have regarding what put and call options are. However, we haven't yet introduced what a strike price is in the world of options trading, so that's what we'll do now before moving on with our discussion about the straddling strategy. With that being said:

Strike price: the price at which the holder of a put or call option can buy or sell an asset; commonly referred to as an exercise price.

Example: Company XYZ's stock ABC is currently trading at $100. The stock shows promise (and constant upwards movement in market value), so you buy a call option with a strike price of $200. This means you maintain the right to purchase Company XYZ's stock ABC for $200, even after the stock's value increases to $350 just five days later. You maintain this right to buy at a pre-established price as long as you do so on or before the call option's expiration date.

If that makes sense, let's go ahead and move forward with our discussion of straddling. So, like we just learned a moment ago, the straddling strategy of options trading involves buying both a put and call option of a stock, with the same strike price and expiration date. Although it seems a bit complicated, all this really means is that you're protected on both sides—if the stock experiences a downward trend in stock value, you can sell at your pre-determined price, and if the stock experiences an upward trend in stock value, you can buy at your pre-determined price.

Straddling is a simple concept, but it tends to get a bit complicated when we merely use words to explain it. So, let's throw some actual numbers out there to help the more visual or math-orientated learners. Here's a scenario that involves the short-term strategy of straddling.

1.) Jane the options trader researches and discovers that stock CDF has experienced a steady upwards trend in price over the last 3 months. In April stock CDF was valued at $20, in May it was valued at $30, and in June it was valued at $40.

2.) Jane decides to approach this investment using the straddling strategy, so she buys both a put and call option for stock CDF in July when stock CDF has a $50 market price. Jane buys both call and put options with a September 1**st** expiration date and a $100 strike price.

Scenario #1:

- In August, stock CDF jumps in market value from $50 to $150. (Remember, Jane has both put and call options for this stock with strike prices of $100 on each).

- Seeing the profit she would generate if she exercised her call option, Jane does so. (Remember: with a call option, Jane has the right to buy an asset at the strike price agreed upon beforehand).

- Jane, using her call option, buys stock CDF (which has a market value of $150), with her strike price of $100. In the process, Jane generates a $50 profit, and exits her position.

Scenario #2:

- In August, stock CDF suddenly falls in market value from $50 to $30. (Again, remember that Jane has both put and call options for this stock with strike prices of $100 each).

- Jane notes the decline in market value, and decides she doesn't want to take any further risks, so she decides to exercise her put option. (Remember: with a put option, Jane has the right to sell an asset at the strike price agreed upon beforehand).

- Jane, using her put option, sells stock CDF (which has a current market value of $30), with her strike price of $100. In the process, Jane generates a $70 profit, and exits her position.

If you haven't yet gathered, the main idea behind straddling is this: a trader always has two options, and when one fails, the other protects against significant loss, and even generates profit. This double-layered protection is ideal for the beginner options trader.

Keep in mind, though, that strike prices require actual money. For simplicity's sake, this is something that I didn't include in the above scenarios, but it's important that you understand what's going on here with strike price. So, Jane bought a call and put option, each with a $100 strike price, right? Well, that was a $200 investment for Jane, since a strike price is essentially what you're paying the other person to "hold" an option opportunity for you. When we factor this into the scenarios, Jane isn't exactly securing a profit, is she? No, she's not. If we were to use this as a real-life scenario, Jane would be better off setting a lower strike price (maybe $40, for example), and waiting until the stock underwent a dramatic upward growth in price. I haven't done that here, though, because I wanted to show you plain and simple how straddling works. But now that you have that understanding for the strategy, I've been able to add one more layer—keeping in mind the initial investment you'll need to make in order to create a strike price.

Nonetheless, the two strategies of married put and straddling come highly recommended, not only by me, but by financial experts and investors who strive to help beginner options traders achieve financial success in the market arena. By understanding and employing these two crucial strategies (though not at the same time), beginner options traders put themselves in a good position.

However, there are further steps you can take to help you secure even greater success and help you generate even larger profit. The suggestions that you'll find below are excellent tips to keep in mind during your first 48 hours of trading and while you use short-term strategies, and both can be **combined** with one another as you use either the married put or straddling strategy.

Moving Averages

All a moving average indicates is the average price of a stock over a certain period of time. Moving averages can take the form of many timeframes, typically from 15 days to 200 days, and the most common timeframes are 20, 30, 50, and 100 days. Although it's quite simple, the moving average of a stock is something you'll want to keep track of quite closely because it provides a great indication of whether a stock is moving in an upwards or downwards trend. (This will help you determine, if you're using the straddling strategy, for example, whether you should exercise either your call or put option).

Moving averages are very easy to get your hands on. You can either 1.) keep track of a stock's market value on your own, and calculate its weekly or monthly moving average on your own as well, or 2.) Refer to stock charts and graphs, which are readily available, and always at your fingertips if you've downloaded a financial app such as:

- ChartIQ Pro

- StockSpy

- Daily Stocks

- WikiInvest Portfolio

If you do decide to keep track of moving averages, whether on your own or using financial tools, keep in mind that moving averages not only indicate when to invest, but when to exit as well. More experienced traders might tell you it's sometimes worth your time to stick around and see what happens if a stock's moving average begins to flatten or decline, though I don't recommend doing so, at least during your first 48 hours of trading when you're just starting out. Exiting an investment is always the safest route to take when stock values flatten or become static. Yes, you might lose out on profitable opportunities if the stock experiences a spike after you've exited, but you're also not taking the risk of losing money if the stock acts in the opposite way and experiences a sudden downwards spike in price.

Cycles and Patterns

If you know anything about the general stock market, it's that it's a highly volatile and unpredictable environment. I mean, it can be genuinely cruel...brutal...harsh. Use whatever word you'd like, but it is. At the same time, however, stocks usually fall under certain patterns and cycles that, when we pay close attention, we can take note of and use to our advantage. When we realize these patterns and cycles, especially those pertaining to our specific stock or future investment opportunity, we can make educated decisions about a stock's future movements, thereby giving us an upper hand in the cruel environment the stock market offers to its participants.

Research is, of course, a huge factor in discovering what these patterns and cycles are. I can't tell you what each and every stock's weekly, monthly, and yearly pattern and/or cycle is, of course, but what I can do is fill you in on a little secret: between November and April, stocks generally experience "gains" and upward trends (small or large), and between May and October, stocks typically undergo declines in price or experience static (unmoving) market statuses.

Again, financial tools and resources, like the apps I listed above, will help you research, learn about, and understand the particular cycles and patterns associated with your stock. I can't stress enough just how important research is during this entire process, even before your first 48 hours in the options trading market begins. Really, it's very crucial to your success, perhaps even more so than the short-term strategies and suggestions we've discussed in this chapter. Really, I mean that.

Chapter 6: Options Trading in the Forex Market

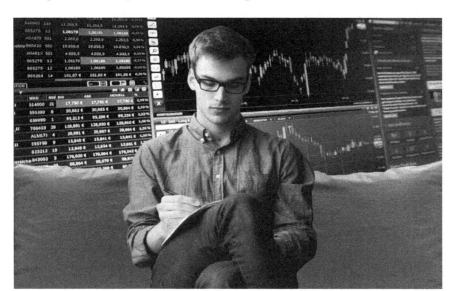

The foreign exchange currency market, or forex as it is typically called, is, without a doubt, the most lucrative investment market in the world. Each day it trades more than 4 trillion dollars which is approximately 10 times as much as the New York Stock Exchange. Despite this massive amount of trading, it was difficult for individual traders to take advantage of the market due to the technological limitations of the time. This is no longer the case; however, as the internet has given rise to numerous forex trading platforms which means that now forex trading is open to everyone.

Unlike many other types of markets, the forex market is purely speculative which means that nothing is actually changing hands when you place a forex trade. Rather, the forex market essentially only exists on various servers and databases worldwide with information coming in from countries all over the world causing these numbers to move in one direction or another. Each transaction is then tracked with any potential losses or a gain expressed in the primary currency of the country the database that is accessing the information is located in.

While this might seem like an odd system, it makes sense when you realize that the only reason the forex market exists is that major corporations and countries needed a way to convert currencies from one type to the other without going through a lot of cumbersome steps to do so. These major players tend to move amounts of currency that are vast enough to affect the actual value of the currencies being traded which is where the speculative portion of the equation comes into play.

Currently, only about 20 percent of the activity related to the forex market comes from these major players with the rest instead of coming from investors who are looking to make money based on the way the various currencies are reacting to the current market. A majority of these traders are professionals who work for financial institutions or hedge funds though more and more freelance traders are jumping on the forex bandwagon every day.

Forex basics: The most important thing to keep in mind when it comes to forex trading is that forex trades always consist of a pair of currency rather than a single asset like you would see in the stock or options market. What this means is that for every trade a forex trader is buying one currency and selling another. Currency is typically traded in 3 differing quantities, known as lots. A micro lot is 1,000 currency units, a mini lot is 10,000 units and a standard lot is 100,000 units.

The smallest amount that a given currency can move is one percent of its current total which is referred to as a pip. When you are first starting out with forex trading then it is recommended that you trade in micro lots as a single pip there is only work 10 cents of the currency in question. This means you will have less at stake during the early days when you are still finding your footing and you may often find yourself fighting against a market that has turned against you in unexpected ways. If you instead start with mini lots then with each pip of movement you are risking $10. To put this into perspective, the market frequently moves 100 pips or more in an average trading session.

While the forex market has several unique features that set it apart from other equities markets, it is the same in the ways that matter the most. Specifically, it is still driven by the core concept of supply and demand. As such, if a certain currency is experiencing high demand, then the value of that currency will increase accordingly until it reaches a point of oversaturation whereupon it will start to move back in the other direction. This means that as a forex trader you are going to need to be aware of when a given currency is going to increase in demand so that you can buy into it at the lowest price possible and thus reap the greatest rewards. This means you will always need to be aware of key interest rate movements, economic predications, and geopolitical strife.

Another important fact to keep in mind is that from Monday morning to Friday evening, the forex market never closes. Despite this fact, currency pairs are typically only traded during the times of day when the country whose currency it is are most active. Each trading day is generally broken into 3 chunks, Europe, US and Asia with the related currency pairs being traded during those periods.

This is the case because the currency pairs of those regions are always going to be more valuable during the periods of prime activity for the region in question. As an example, if you were thinking about trading a pair based around the US dollar and the Japanese yen then you would find that pair to be most profitable during the US hours and again during the Asian hours.

While there is currency pairs for essentially every combination of currency imaginable, the majority of forex trading can be broken down into 18 primary pairs. These 18 pairs are, in turn, made up of just 8 currencies that you are going to need to be familiar with if you hope to find success in the forex market. These are AUD the Australian dollar, CAD the Canadian dollar, CHF the Swiss franc, EUR the euro, GBP the British pound, JPY the Japanese yen, NZD the New Zealand dollar and USD the US dollar. Knowing what currencies to focus on and which to ignore, at least up front, is crucial to making the early days of forex trading as manageable as possible. There will be plenty of time for exploring lesser used currencies later, once you are completely comfortable with the basics.

Short-term strategy: If you are interested in trading options in the forex market in the short term then it is important to keep in mind that your goal should always be to control the amount of risk you take on as much as possible. This will make it easier for you to deal in charts that tend to offer shorter time frames than many forex traders deal in. This doesn't mean that you are going to want to stick to the short-term charts exclusively, however, as this can cause your profits to be lower overall than they would otherwise be.

To trade effectively in the short-term, the first thing you are going to want to be on the lookout for is a pair of moving averages on the hourly charts. The trading platform that you use should be able to automatically generate what you are looking for based on the timeframe that you choose. After you have the indicators that you are looking for, you will then be able to more easily utilize them as a sort of guidepost that will make it easier to determine how the market is moving in the timeframe in question so that you will be able to look before you leap as it were. If the resulting short moving average is less than the larger moving average then you will want to take a long position, otherwise, you will want to take a short position instead.

Once you have determined the trend that you are looking for, the next thing you will need to do is to look at the entries that are going to match the direction of the trend you are following. The goal here should be to successfully locate the momentum that you saw on the longer chart in either the 15-minute or 5-minute chart that you will actually want to do work in.

When putting this strategy to use, it is crucial that you keep in mind that it will not always be the right time to buy in. Instead, you are going to need to be patient and wait for a position that is profitable to open up and the best way to do so is to look for the exponential moving average. When seeking out the exponential moving average you are going to want to start by finding a trigger known as the 8-period exponential on the 5-minute chart which should be available from your trading platform. When this exponential starts to move in the direction of the trend you are following then you will know that it is a good time to go ahead and buy in.

While this strategy requires a good deal of micromanaging in order to be successful, it is also beneficial in several ways. The first of which is that if you choose to wait until you see the right trigger then you know that other traders are already creating action around the currency pair in question which means you can be fairly certain that the trade will be profitable. Additionally, this is a great strategy to use for those who have a lower amount of starter capital as it will make it easier to jump in on a given currency pair before the momentum picks up steam and the bullish nature of the pair causes the price to raise to a less tantalizing point.

In addition to making it easy to buy cheap, those who use this strategy when it comes to selling currency pairs they currently own will be able to do so to maximize their profits as they will be able to get out of a given trade before the masses do so, thus ensuring a higher price when they sell. It is important to remember, however, that the price could instead experience a short-term retracement which means you need to be sure of what the signals are telling you before you make a move if you don't want to pay the price for jumping out early.

In order to ensure a level of maximum profit with this strategy, you are going to need to set your stop losses at such a point that they are just underneath the last high that the currency experienced. If you are investing in short positions then you will want to set your stop losses so they are just above the current low price point instead. This will ensure that you don't lose out if the trend loses momentum before it reaches the price you are hoping for. By doing so you ensure that the short-term strategy remains as versatile as possible.

This strategy is not without risks of its own, however, as the short-term charts are prone to changing dramatically with little or no advanced notice. This means that if you hope to profit when using this strategy, you are going to need to make sure that you have the ability to react quickly to unexpected changes. The best reaction most of the time is going to be waiting for the currency to settle down before setting a new stop loss based on the new landscape that is slightly in the money without getting greedy.

Fibonacci retracement: To use a Fibonacci retracement, the first thing you are going to want to look for is a market that is trending. The general idea here is to go long on a retracement, a temporary reversal of direction in the price of the currency, at a specific level when the market is positively trending and to go short on retracements when the market is trending in the other direction. To find a retracement level you are going to want to find moments when pricing indicators you are looking for reach high, or low, points that are higher, or lower, than the average high, or low, point.

To understand the Fibonacci ratios that are useful in forex, it is important to understand the basics behind the Fibonacci numbers which were discovered by the man whose name they bear; they start off as 0, 1, 2, 3, 5, 7, 13, 21, etc. Essentially, to find the next number in the sequence you simply add the previous 2 numbers in the sequence together. Now, if you measure the ratio of each number to the following number in the sequence you get the Fibonacci ratios that are used in forex. These start off as .236, .382, .5, .618 etc. While the exact reason that Fibonacci ratios apply to the forex market isn't completely clear, it is clear that they resonate throughout the world at large from the smallest instance in individual molecules of DNA to the grandest in the organization of the planets in the sky.

Luckily, when it comes to utilizing the Fibonacci ratio in your trades, you don't need to memorize these numbers as all forex trading platforms will have a tool that will do the calculations for you. This means that all you really need to do is to learn how, when and why to use them in a technical analysis sense. It is important to keep in mind that Fibonacci levels are going to act as resistance as well as support for the price in question. As the price increases, the Fibonacci levels will act as resistance and as the price decreases, they will act as support. Additionally, much like with regular support or resistance they can be broken.

Trades that are based around the Fibonacci retracement on the charts for timeframes less than 10 minutes. Fibonacci retracements can be used to determine reasonable reward/risk levels either by selling a credit spread to the level in question or through buying options that are already in the money that are likely to experience a bounce at these levels. It is generally going to be in your best interest to look for Fibonacci levels that are likely to overlap at multiple timeframes as well as corresponding to the most recent trend experienced by the underlying stock. If you are so inclined, you can also utilize candlestick price patterns as a means of confirming a buy at specific Fibonacci levels.

Alternately, you may find success with oversold or overbought indicators when it comes to range-bound or trendless stocks. You can then sell credit spreads or buy into options that are already in the money and near the current level of resistance and support with tight stops. It is important to keep in mind that a given stock might not move quickly enough to make these levels worthwhile so it is important to do your research ahead of time in order to have a reasonable expectation about the future movement.

Indicators that are used to signal lower than average volatility such as Bollinger bands are especially useful when it comes to place trades that you anticipate big moves from. Breakout indicators time, especially for the shorter charts, is also especially useful.

Using the Fibonacci sequence to perform a retracement gives you the ability to determine how much an asset moved at price initially. It uses multiple horizontal lines to point out resistance or support at 23.6, 38.2, 50, 61.8 or 100 percent. When used properly they make it easier to identify the spots transactions should be started, what prices to target and what stop losses to set.

This doesn't mean that you should apply the Fibonacci retracements blindly as doing so can lead to failure as easily as it can success. It is important to avoid choosing inconsistent reference points which can easily lead to mistakes as well as misanalysis, for example, mistaking the wick for the body of a candle. Retracements using the Fibonacci sequence should always be applied wick-to-wick which in turn leads to a clearly defined and actionable resistance level.

Likewise, it is important to always keep the big picture in mind and keep an eye on trends that are of the longer variety as well. Failing to keep a broad perspective in mind makes short-term trades more likely to fail as it makes it harder to project the correct momentum and direction any potential opportunities might be moving in. Keeping the larger trends in mind will help you pick more reliable trades while also preventing you from accidentally trading against a specific trend.

Don't forget, Fibonacci retracements are likely to indicate quality trades, but they will never be able to do so in a complete vacuum. It is best to start with a retracement and then apply other tools including stochastic oscillators or MACD. Moving ahead without confirmation will leave you with little except positive thoughts and wishes that the outcome goes the way you want. Remember, there is no one indicator that is strong enough to warrant moving forward on a trade without double checking the validity of the data.

The other limitation of a Fibonacci retracement is that it doesn't work reliably over shorter time frames as there is simply too much interference from standard market volatility which will result in false apparent levels of support as well as resistance. What's more, the addition of whipsaws and spikes can make it difficult to utilize stops effectively which can result in tight and narrow confluences.

Chapter 7: The Option Pricing Models

The option premium is the actual price paid by the option holder for his right to exercise the option before it expires. This amount is paid to the option writer or seller. On the other hand, the option's theoretical value is the estimated option value, which is computed through a price model. It is the current value of the option that includes all factors, which change during the life of the option.

An option trader can use different price models to compute for the theoretical value. These models have forecasted and fixed values. Each of the variables can fluctuate over the option's lifetime. A lot of investors and traders use the updated theoretical value to monitoring the fluctuating value and risk of the option. They don't have to compute it by themselves. A lot of trading platforms offer updated values. There are also different websites which offer theoretical value calculators.

The Black-Scholes Model

As a method for computing option premium, it was published in the Journal of Political Economy as a paper entitled "The Pricing of Options and Corporate Liabilities". Two years after Black passed away, Merton and Scholes received the Nobel Prize in Economics in 1997 for their work. The option pricing model is used to compute the theoretical price of European call and put options and ignores any dividends paid during the life of the option. However, it is currently being adapted to take into consideration the dividends by determining the value on the ex-dividend date of the underlying asset.

The Black-Scholes option pricing model assumes that the options are exercised only on the date of expiration and the underlying asset doesn't pay out dividends during the lifetime of the options. Furthermore, it assumes that the price movements of the market are unpredictable. No commissions are also taken into consideration. The Black-Scholes model also assumes that the underlying asset's volatility and the risk-free rate are constant and known.

Lastly, the returns of the underlying asset follow a normal distribution.

The Black-Scholes option pricing model may be intimidating and complicated to a lot of investors. However, these investors and traders don't need to know how to compute by themselves because there are various option price calculators available online. In fact, even option trading platforms offer these calculators. An investor only needs to know 5 variables: the risk-free interest rate, the number of days before expiration, the price of the underlying asset, and the option strike price.

The Cox-Rubenstein Binomial Option Pricing Model

This pricing model is a variation of the Black-Scholes pricing model. Proposed by John Carrington Cox, Mark Edward Rubenstein, and Stephen Ross in 1979, this model became popular because the lattice-based model is used in considering the price of the underlying asset over a period of time. This lattice-based model considers the expected changes in different factors over the life of the option. As such, it produces a more accurate estimate of the option price. The Cox-Rubenstein Binomial model is used for American options, which can be exercised anytime until they expire.

Using a risk-neutral valuation, the Cox-Ross-Rubenstein option pricing model assumes that everyone is indifferent to risk and that the world is risk neutral. As such, the possible returns are the same as the risk-free interest rate. The model further assumes that arbitrage isn't possible and that for each period the price of the underlying asset can never go in opposite directions at the same time. It uses an iterative structure which specifies the time nodes between the present and the date of option expiration. It offers a mathematical valuation which creates a binomial tree where all possible values at various nodes are represented.

This pricing model assumes that the price of the underlying asset can only go up or down until the option expires. The price valuation starts with every final node and iteration are performed from the expiration date backwards up to the valuation date. It involves 3 steps: creation of the binomial tree; calculation of the value of the option at every final node; and calculation of the option value at every preceding node. The Cox-Ross-Rubenstein model is less complicated. However, like the Black-Scholes model, users can avail of the different online calculators. Trading online platforms also offer tools to compute the price values.

The Put/Call Parity

In his "The Relation between Put and Call Prices" paper in 1969, Hans Stoll defined the interconnection between the European call and put options with the same strike price and expiration. The call option price is the put option's fair value at a particular strike price. This relation came to be because the options' combinations created positions which were similar to the underlying asset's position. For this to hold true, both underlying asset and option positions must have the same arbitrage or return opportunity. Investors and traders can profit from this arbitrage, without risk, up to the point when the parity returned. Arbitrage allows the investor to profit from the differences in price of one underlying asset in various markets. As in illustration, if the trader buys a share of stock for $45 from one market while he simultaneously sell the same stock in another market for $50. This synchronized transaction can allow him to generate a profit from the trade with little or no risk.

In order to replicate the long position of an underlying asset, an investor can have a short put option and a long call option simultaneously. On the other hand, a short position of the underlying asset can be replicated by have a long put option and a short call option simultaneously. If the parity doesn't exit, the investor can profit from the arbitrage opportunities. An option trader can test the European option pricing model through the put/call parity. If the prices of put and call options don't satisfy parity, it means that there is an arbitrage opportunity. As such, the pricing model must be rejected.

For a non-dividend paying underlying asset, the following formula can be used to determine the option price:

$c = S + p - Xe - r(T - t)$

$p = c - S + Xe - r(T - t)$

Where:

c = value of the call option

S = current price of the underlying asset

p = value of the put option

X = strike price

e = Euler's constant (2.71828)

r = risk-free interest rate; compounded continuously

T = option expiry date

t = current valuation date

There are a lot of trading platforms which offer this tool. Some of these providers also offer put/call parity visual representations.

Profit And Loss Diagrams

A risk graph or profit and loss diagram is a graphical representation of an option strategy's potential profit and loss at a given time. An option trader can use this diagram to determine how his strategy can perform over different prices so that he can understand possible outcomes. To create the diagram, the prices of the underlying asset are plotted along the horizontal axis while the potential profit and loss numbers are then plotted along the vertical axis. The profits are plotted above the breakeven point while the losses are found below it. The resulting line graph represents the possible profit and loss on the range of prices of the underlying asset.

The Greek Values

The Delta computes for the sensitivity of the option price to fluctuations in the price of the underlying asset. It is an important Greek value because it indicates how the price of the option will move in relation to the price change of the underlying asset. Its value can range from 0 to 1 for call options. For put options, the value can move from 0 to

-1. The delta value can also be represented from 0 to 100 for call options and 0 to -100 for put options so that decimals won't be used. An out-of-the-money call option can have deltas nearing 0. An in-the-money call option can have deltas nearing 1.

The Vega is a measure of the sensitivity of the price of the option to volatility changes of the underlying asset. It represents the changes of the option price to a 1% volatility change of the underlying asset. If there's still more time before the option expires, an increase in the volatility of the asset can have a greater impact on the option price. If there is an increased volatility, it means that the underlying asset may experience extreme values. Any increase in the volatility will have a corresponding increase in the option price. On the other hand, any decrease in the volatility will have its corresponding decrease in the option value.

The Gamma measures delta sensitivity in relation to the price fluctuations of the underlying asset. It measures the change in delta in response to every change in price of the underlying asset. Because deltas change at various rates, gamma measures and analyzes delta. It is useful in the determination of the stability of the delta. If the gamma results to a high value, it means that the delta can vary dramatically in relation to a small price movement of the underlying asset. An at-the-money option will give a high gamma. A low gamma is a result of an out-of-the-money or in-the-money option. If there's still a lot of time before the option expires, the gamma is low because the option is less sensitive to the changes in the delta. However, as the expiration date draws near, the gamma goes higher because changes in the delta have more impact.

The theta is a measure of the option's time decay, which is a theoretical value that the option may lose daily as it nears its expiration date. An at-the-money option increases the theta value while an out-of-the-money or in-the-money option decreases it. Long call and put options have negative thetas while short call and put options have positive thetas. A zero theta can result if the value of the underlying asset isn't depreciated by time.

Chapter 8: Fundamental Analysis

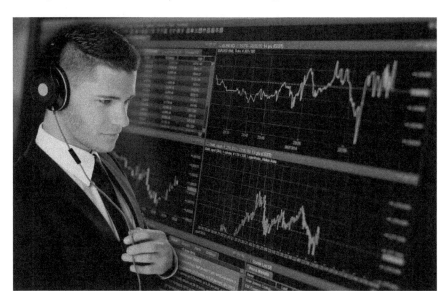

While it should come as no surprise that you are going to need to gather as much data as possible in order to make the best trades, regardless of what market you are working in; it is important to keep in mind that if you don't use it in the right way then it is all for naught. There are two ways to get the most out of any of the data that you gather, the first is via technical analysis and the second is via fundamental analysis. As a general rule, you will likely find it helpful to start off with fundamental analysis before moving on to technical analysis as the need arises.

To understand the difference between the two you may find it helpful to think about technical analysis as analyzing charts while fundamental analysis looks at specific factors based on the underlying asset for the market that you are working in. The core tenant of fundamental analysis is that there are related details out there that can tell the whole story when it comes to the market in question while technical analysis believes that the only details that are required are those that relate to the price at the moment. As such, fundamental analysis is typically considered easier to master as it all relates to concepts less expressly related to understanding market movement exclusively. Meanwhile, technical analysis is typically faster because key fundamental analysis data often is only made publicly available on a strict, and limited, schedule, sometimes only a few times a year meaning the availability for updating specific data is rather limited.

Fundamental Analysis Rules

The best time to use fundamental analysis is when you are looking to gain a broad idea of the state of the market as it stands and how that relates to the state of things in the near future when it comes time to actually trading successfully. Regardless of what market you are considering, the end goals are the same, find the most effective trade for the time period that you are targeting.

Establish a baseline: In order to begin analyzing the fundamentals, the first thing that you will need to do is to create a baseline regarding the company's overall performance. In order to generate the most useful results possible, the first thing that you are going to need to do is to gather data both regarding the company in question as well as the related industry as a whole. When gathering macro data, it is important to keep in mind that no market is going to operate in a vacuum which means the reasons behind specific market movement can be much more far reaching than they first appear. Fundamental analysis works because of the stock market's propensity for patterns which means if you trace a specific market movement back to the source you will have a better idea of what to keep an eye on in the future.

Furthermore, all industries go through several different phases where their penny stocks are going to be worth more or less overall based on general popularity. If the industry is producing many popular penny stocks, then overall volatility will be down while at the same time liquidity will be at an overall high.

Consider worldwide issues: Once you have a general grasp on the current phase you are dealing with, the next thing you will want to consider is anything that is going on in the wider world that will after the type of businesses you tend to favor in your penny stocks. Not being prepared for major paradigm shifts, especially in penny stocks where new companies come and go so quickly, means that you can easily miss out on massive profits and should be avoided at all costs.

To ensure you are not blindsided by news you could have seen coming, it is important to look beyond the obvious issues that are consuming the 24-hour news cycle and dig deeper into the comings and goings of the nations that are going to most directly affect your particular subsection of penny stocks. One important worldwide phenomenon that you will want to pay specific attention to is anything in the realm of technology as major paradigm shifts like the adoption of the smartphone, or the current move towards electric cars can create serious paradigm shifts.

Put it all together: Once you have a clear idea of what the market should look like as well as what may be on the horizon, the next step is to put it all together to compare what has been and what might to what the current state of the market is. Not only will this give you a realistic idea of what other investors are going to do if certain events occur the way they have in the past, you will also be able to use these details in order to identify underlying assets that are currently on the cusp of generating the type of movement that you need if you want to utilize them via binary option trades.

The best time to get on board with a new underlying asset is when it is nearing the end of the post-bust period or the end of a post-boom period depending on if you are going to place a call or a put. In these scenarios, you are going to have the greatest access to the freedom of the market and thus have the access to the greatest overall allowable risk that you are going to find in any market. Remember, the amount of risk that you can successfully handle without an increase in the likelihood of failure is going to start decreasing as soon as the boom or bust phase begins in earnest so it is important to get in as quickly as possible if you hope to truly maximize your profits.

Understand the relative strength of any given trade: When an underlying asset is experiencing a boom phase, the strength of its related fundamentals is going to be what determines the way that other investors are going to act when it comes to binary options trading. Keeping this in mind it then stands to reason that the earlier a given underlying asset is in a particular boom phase, the stronger the market surrounding it is going to be. Remember, when it comes to fundamental analysis what an underlying asset looks like at the moment isn't nearly as important as what it is likely to look like in the future and the best way to determine those details is by keeping an eye on the past.

Quantitative Fundamental Analysis

The sheer volume of data and a large amount of varying numbers found in the average company's financial statements can easily be intimidating and bewildering for conscientious investors who are digging into them for the first time. Once you get the hang of them, however, you will quickly find that they are a goldmine of information when it comes to determining how likely a company is to continue producing reliable dividends in the future.

At their most basic, a company's financial statements disclose the information relating to its financial performance over a set period of time. Unlike with qualitative concepts, financial statements provide cold, hard facts about a company that is rarely open for interpretation.

Important statements

Balance sheet: A balance sheet shows a detailed record of all of a company's equity, liabilities and assets for a given period of time. A balance sheet shows a balance to the financial structure of a company by dividing the company's equity by the combination of shareholders and liabilities in order to determine its current assets.

In this case, assets represent the resources that the company is actively in control of at a specific point in time. It can include things like buildings, machinery, inventory, cash and more. It will also show the total value of any financing that has been used to generate those assets. Financing can come from either equity or liabilities. Liabilities include debt that must be paid back eventually while equity, in this case, measures the total amount of money that its owners have put into the business. This can include profits from previous years, which are known collectively as retained earnings.

Income statement: While the balance sheet can be thought of as a snapshot of the fundamental economic aspects of the company, an income statement takes a closer look at the performance of the company exclusively for a given timeframe. There is no limit to the length of time an income statement considers, which means you could see them generated month to month, or even day to day; however, the most common type used by public companies are either annual or quarterly. Income statements provide information on profit, expenses, and revenues that resulted from the business that took place over the specific period of time.

Cash flow statement: The cashflow statement frequently shows all of the cash outflow and inflow for the company over a given period of time. The cash flow statement often focuses on operating cash flow which is the cash that will be generated by day to day business operations. It will also include any cash that is available from investing which is often used as a means of investing in assets along with any cash that might have been generated by long-term asset sales or the sale of a secondary business that the company previously owned. Cash due to financing is another name for money that is paid off or received based on issuing or borrowing funds.

While accountants can manipulate earnings with ease, it is much more difficult to fake having access to cash in the bank where there is none that really exists. This is why many savvy investors consider the cash flow statement the most reliable way to measure a specific company's performance.

Finding the details: While tracking down all the disparate financial statements on the company's you are considering purchasing stock in can be cumbersome, the Securities and Exchange Commission (SEC) requires all publicly traded companies to submit regular filings outlining all of their financial activities including a variety of different financial statements. This also includes information such as managerial discussions, reports from auditors, deep dives into the operations and prospects of upcoming years and more.

These types of details can all be found in the 10-K filing that each company is required to file every year, along with the 10-Q filing that they must send out once per quarter. Both types of documents can be found online, both at the corporate website for the company as well as on the SEC website. As the version that hits the corporate site doesn't need to be complete, it is best to visit SEC.gov and get to know the Electronic Data Gathering, Analysis, and Retrieval system (EDGAR) which automates the process of indexing, validating, collecting, forward and accepting submissions. As this system was designed in the mid-90s, however, it is important to dedicate some time to learning the process as it is more cumbersome than 20 years of user interface advancements have to lead you to expect.

Qualitative Fundamental Analysis

Qualitative factors are generally less tangible and include things like its name recognition, the patents it holds and the quality of its board members. Qualitative factors to consider include:

Business model: The first thing that you are going to want to do when you catch wind of a company that might be worth following up on is to check out its business model which is more or less a generalization of how it makes its money. You can typically find these sorts of details on the company website or in its 10-K filing.

Competitive advantage: It is also important to consider the various competitive advantages that the company you have your eye on might have over its competition. Companies that are going to be successful in the long-term are always going to have an advantage over their competition in one of two ways. They can either have better operational effectiveness or improved strategic positioning. Operational effectiveness is the name given to doing the same things as the competition but in a more efficient and effective way. Strategic positioning occurs when a company gains an edge by doing things that nobody else is doing.

Changes to the company: In order to properly narrow down your search, you will typically find the most reliable results when it comes to companies that have recently seen major changes to their corporate structure as it is these types of changes that are likely to ultimately precede events that are more likely to see the company jump to the next level. The specifics of what happened in this instance are nearly as important as the fact that statistically speaking, 95 percent of companies that experience this type of growth started with a significant change to the status quo.

Chapter 9: Technical Indicators

Technical indicators come into play in options trading when you need to determine turning points for underlying stock and the trends that get them to this point. When used correctly, they can help to determine the optimal time to buy or sell and also predict movement cycles. In general, technical indicators are calculated based on the pricing pattern of the underlying stock. Relevant data includes highs and lows, opening price, volume and closing price. They typically take into account the data regarding a stock's price from the past few periods, based on the charts the person who is doing the analyzing prefers.

This information is then used to identify trends that show what has been happening regarding a specific stock and then using past information to determine likely results for the future. Technical indicators come in both leading and lagging varieties. Indicators that lag are based on data that already exists and make it easier to determine if a trend is in the process of forming or if the stock in question is simply trading within a range. The stronger the trend that the lagging indicator pinpoints the greater the chance it is going to continue into the future. They typically drop the ball when it comes to predicting potential pullbacks or rally points, however.

When it comes to leading indicators, they are mainly useful when you are looking to predict the point in the future where the price of a specific stock is going to crash or rally. More often than not, these are going to be momentum indicators which, as the name implies, gauge the strength of the movement the underlying stock is going to undertake. Leading indicators tend to come in handy when you need to determine if the price the stock in question has reached is untenable in the long run and, if so, when the slowdown of the current trend is likely to occur. Because both oversold and overbought stocks are guaranteed to experience a pullback, knowing when this move is going to occur will come in handy more likely than not.

Both types of indicators are equally useful at different times, and often in conjunction with one another as you will frequently need to know both what types of trends are forming and when they are ultimately going to peter out if you are going to want to utilize most strategies successfully. In general, you are going to want to stick to a minimum of 3 indicators at all times.

Moving average convergence divergence indicator: The moving average convergence divergence (MACD) indicator is a type of oscillating indicator that generally moves between the centerline and zero. If the MACD value is high, then this indicates the related stock is close to being overbought, and if the value is low then the stock is in danger of being oversold.

MACD charts are generally based on a combination of multiple exponential moving averages (EMAs). These averages can be based on any time frame, though the most common is the 12-26-9 chart. This chart is typically broken into multiple parts, the first of which is the 26-day and 12-day chart. Using an EMA that is slower or fast allows you to more accurately gauge the current momentum level for the trend you are currently keeping an eye on.

If the 12-day EMA, the fast of the pair, ends up being above the 26-day EMA then you can safely assume that the underlying stock is in an uptrend while the reverse will also be the case. If the 12-day EMA increases at a rate that is greater than the 26-day EMA, then the uptrend is generally going to be even more pronounced. IF the 12-day EMA starts to move closer to the 26-day, then you can accurately assume that it is slowing down which means the momentum of the trade is going to fade. This, in turn, means you should expect the uptrend to end shortly.

The MACD puts these EMAs to use by considering the difference between them and then plotting it out. If the 26-day and the 12-day end up being the same, then the MACD will equal out to 0. If the 12-day ends up at a higher point than the 26-day, then the MACD will end up being positive. Otherwise, it will be negative. The larger the difference between them, the further the MACD line will fall from zero if the result is negative or from the center line if the result is positive.

By itself, this line does not provide any information that you would not be able to find from a simple moving average. However, it becomes much more useful once the 9-day EMA is taken into account as well. The 9-day EMA is different from the other 2 in that it shows the trend of the

MACD line rather than the stock price. This means the 9-day EMA smooth's out the movement of the MACD line to make its results more manageable.

In addition to the 9-day EMA, you are also going to want to look at the MACD histogram which looks at the difference between it and the base MACD line. When the MACD line crosses above the 9-day EMA, the MACD histogram will typically cross above 0 and thus indicate a bullish signal. If it crosses on the other side of 0, then you can take that to indicate a trend that will turn bearish if it has not already. When put to a chart, the histogram will form in a series of peak that descends if the underlying stock is experiencing negative divergence and will generate a series of ascending peaks if it is experiencing positive divergence.

If the result generates a trend indicating negative divergence then you can feel relatively certain that the current positive trend is going to hit a level of resistance that it will not be able to overcome and, thus, reverse sooner than later. This can happen even if the pattern of the underlying stock has not started to run out of momentum quite yet. The same can be said about positive divergence and a negative trend. Remember the fact that these signals can become muddied if the price trades at or near the maximum range for a prolonged period. This means for the best results you are always going to want to use multiple indicators at once to prevent yourself from giving in to false signals.

Average directional index: The average directional index can be thought of as a guidepost that confirms the signals that other technical indicators bring to light. After a trend has been identified successfully, the average directional index can then more easily determine its strength compared to the other trends that are currently taking place. The average directional index is a combination of directional indicators that are both negative and positive and thus can more easily track trends regardless of their direction. They are then unified in a way that determines the overall strength of the trend.

As an oscillating indicator, the average directional index ranges between 100 and 0. The low end indicates that the trend is essentially flat and without volatility while the high end indicates that the stock is virtually moving straight up and down very quickly. This indicator is only useful when it comes to measuring the overall strength of the trend, not which direction it is moving in or is likely to move in anytime soon.

As a general rule, it is rare to see an average directional index value above 60. This is because trends with that much strength are only likely to appear in periods of deep recession or extremely long bullish market runs. What this means is that a value of anything greater than 40 can be considered a vibrant trend and anything lower than 20 indicates an underlying stock within a trading range.

When watching for average directional index signals, if a trend moves from above 40 to below it, then you can assume the current trend is slowing which means it may be time to mix up your current trading strategy or close out any existing positions. However, if you see a trend start at less than 20 and then increase to a point near 40 then you will know that a neutral market is starting to pick up steam and a major trend is likely going to be formed.

It is also important to always keep in mind the point where the negative directional index and the positive directional index cross. If the negative directional index is crossed by the positive in an upward direction, then you can assume the market is feeling bullish. If things happen the other way, then you can expect bearish trends instead.

Relative strength index: The relative strength index (RSI) is another type of momentum indicator that compares the relative magnitude of recent losses when compared to recent gains as a means of determining if a given stock is oversold or overbought. This, in turn, allows it to generate vital indications about the correlating reversals or corrections that are forthcoming, making price movements in the short-term clearer. RSI is most effective when used to measure individual stocks as opposed to indexes because it is more likely the individuals will experience either condition.

RSI values range from 0 to 100. Any value above 70 shows the stock is overbought and anything under 30 shows it is undersold. In general, options that are on high beta stocks with high liquidity are going to provide the best RSI results.

Some traders find that the RSI provides the most effective information when it is compared to crossovers with the short-term moving average. With the help of a 25-day and a 10-day moving average, you will likely be able to easily discern crossovers that show that a direction shift will occur in periods where the RSI is either in the range of 80 and 20 or 70 and 30. Regardless of what it shows, the RSI is always going to indicate a period of reversal, regardless of the precise direction.

The concept known as failure swings can make it easier for investors to take full advantage of the information shown through an RSI. Remember that just because the RSI shows either something in the range of 30 or 70, does not mean that the reversal is going to happen right away.

Rather, positions can remain in overbought or oversold positions for an extended period. When the RSI extends to these levels, you are going to want to start watching the volume indicators to make it clear when traders start taking profits at the top or building up at the bottom. To make the most of this tool, it may be helpful to study old charts as a means of determining the types of price action you are likely to see at the opposite ends of an RSI, so you know what to expect.

Bollinger Bands: The importance of volatility when it comes to correctly valuing an option is well known. This is why Bollinger bands are as useful as they make it easy to grasp this facet of a particular stock, in turn, making it easier to identify lower and upper ranges. They work by generating bands based on the way the stock price has recently been moving. Bollinger bands tend to provide 2 types of indications:

- The bands tend to contract and expand depending on how volatility decreases or increases based on the way the price has been moving recently. If the bands expand then volatility is increasing, if they contract then volatility is decreasing. With this in mind, you can feel safer taking on reversal based option positions.

- The range of the current band can also be compared to the current market price as a means of determining any potential breakout patterns. If the breakout occurs at the top of the band, then you know the market has been overbought which means it is time to buy puts or short existing calls. If the breakout occurs at the bottom of the lower band, then you know the market is oversold which means it is time to buy short puts or calls that come with lower overall volatility.

- Either way, it is important to take care to assure the current volatility as shorting options if volatility is high can be beneficial. It can lead to higher premiums if volatility is high and cheaper options if volatility is low. The best value for a Bollinger band is up to the trader. However, the most commonly used value is 2 for the standard deviation of the top and bottom bands and 12 for the simple moving average.

The squeeze is the core concept of Bollinger bands as when the bands come close together they constrict the moving average and squeeze it tight, hence the name. A squeeze indicates that the volatility is going to be low for a time while the future likelihood is going to be increased, as will the number of potentially profitable opportunities to trade. On the other hand, the wider the bands end up being, the greater the likelihood of decreased volatility and the higher the likelihood that it is time to exit the trade. Always note that these two conditions are not trading signals in the traditional sense. The bands themselves give no true indication of what direction the price is likely to move in or when the potential change will take place.

Overall, Bollinger bands are not designed to be used in a vacuum. Rather, they are better served as an additional indicator which can then provide traders with additional information when it comes to the volatility of price. Ideally, you will want to use them with at least 2 other indicators that are non-correlated and also provide market signals that are more direct. Using Bollinger bands under these circumstances will help you to discover opportunities that you may have otherwise missed with an overall higher degree of success.

If the value drops, then this indicates a bullish trend which means more calls are being used. Likewise, a value that increases in value is going to show a trend towards bearishness and more puts overall.

As it is dependent on data regarding volume, the MFI indicator is especially useful for options trading based on stocks as opposed to indices. It is also known to see better results for longer forms of options trading than with intraday trading. In general, you will want to look for scenarios where the MFI indicator moves away from the stock price as this is generally a leading indicator that signals a trend reversal is coming. The best values to base your predictions on are going to be 20 for oversold and 80 for overbought.

There are two primary types of financial instruments, these include the primary securities and instruments as well as other instruments whose value is wholly derived based on their relationship to the primary instruments. When it comes to options, those underlying assets are securities which are what this indicator is looking at.

Chapter 10: Open Interests in Options Trading

Open interest reflects the strength of the market. It denotes the number of people interested in a particular trade. This is a very important number. Suppose a stock has been rising continuously but there are no open interests in that stock; it may mean that people are losing interest in that stock. You might face a problem with that stock as nothing can keep moving indefinitely without the active participation of the market.

Open interests provide a strong footing to any stock. It doesn't matter whether the stock is falling or rising, a large number of people interested in that stock will keep it alive and kicking in the market.

We can consider 4 scenarios to understand open interests

1. The prices of a particular trade are rising steadily. People are showing interest in that trade. This means the market is strong.

2. If the prices of a particular trade are falling continuously but people are still showing interest in it then it is a bad sign for the market. This will weaken the market and the prices will continue to fall.

3. If the prices of a trade are rising but people are not showing interest in that trade then it shows that the market has started weakening. This is a red flag.

4. If the prices of a particular trade start falling but there is a lack of open interest in that stock then this means the market is strengthening. People are more inclined towards buying than shorting the trades. It is a positive sign.

A good understanding of the open interests in the market will help you in speculating the trend of the market. It is an important factor and will help you in navigating the market safely.

You must understand that your guess cannot be much better than the guess of hundreds of others who are managing this market. The other thing is that the market runs on the sentiments, it doesn't really run on logic. If a thousand people are thinking something will make money then, believe me, it is already making money.

To take advantage and make money in the opposite market then either you have to be a genius or have some really good backing with a plan.

If you don't have any of these then it is safe to see the mood of the market and act accordingly.

Open interests give power to any stock. They keep the trades alive. Transactions keep ticking.

However, there is also another viewpoint on open interests. Some experts believe that open interests reflect the confidence of the option sellers. If there is any particular option trade that has a great number of open interests, then it wouldn't be hidden from the eyes of the option sellers. Selling a call option is a risk the seller takes. But it is not a blind risk. It is an informed risk. There are several calculations behind it. The seller knows with great accuracy that those levels wouldn't be tested. Otherwise, the losses would become unmanageable. It can happen once in a while, but the same thing occurring repeatedly can ruin any option seller. So, just following the open interests blindly can be very misleading.

Open interests reflect the mood of the market. They show that a stock is being actively traded on the stock exchange.

They also show the confidence of the buyers and the sellers on the stock.

Making the final deductions based on these facts will always be your prerogative.

Chapter 11: Ensuring the Benefits Outweigh the Risks

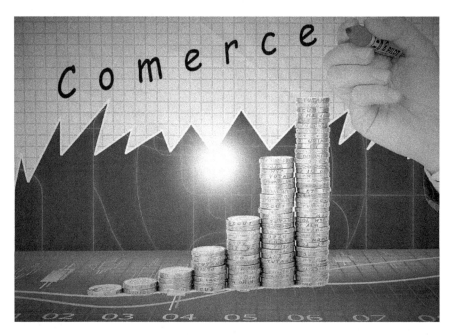

If you've been thinking about investing, have done some preliminary research, or have even had casual conversations with friends and family about investing opportunities, then I'm sure you've stumbled upon the popular topic regarding the benefits and risks of investing and, to be more specific, options trading. I know many of you are probably nodding in agreement (and perhaps experiencing a profound sense of boredom as I bring forth this topic), so you'll be happy to know that I won't be spending too much time on this topic.

If you've had the (fortunate or unfortunate, depends on your take) pleasure of **not** receiving an earful about the benefits and risks of options trading, then you'll find this chapter and the conversation in it to be of some importance.

Benefits

Rather than construct long-winded paragraphs that elaborate on the benefits of options trading, I've decided to forego the long discussion and, instead, include a simple but hopefully comprehensive list that advises readers about the many spectacular benefits they stand to gain by pursuing options. Keep in mind, though, that all of the following benefits won't come immediately, and for some traders, may never come, even. The benefits you receive from options trading depend upon your approach, your experience, your patience, and your dedication, so it's a nearly impossible task to predict which ones will grace your presence. But because you're a beginner trader, simply becoming familiar with the possible benefits of options trading is enough, at least in regards to your initial 48 hours of trading. (Because let's face it, you probably won't experience many of these benefits within your first 48 hours of trading. Many will come for sure, just not so soon).

Here's the list of options trading benefits that you can peruse on your own time:

- Call and put options, along with strike prices and premiums, allow traders not only to take calculated risks, but to have an idea of worst case scenario situations at all times. This lets you **plan ahead,** to gather some sort of idea for what to expect, and to prepare yourself for whatever situation you're confronted with.

- Options have "leverage," which means buying options can help an investor earn more per dollar than buying equity on a stock.

- Risk is significantly reduced with options— any potential for monetary loss is limited to the premium/strike price, so you won't be entirely affected if assets experience a dramatic loss in market value.

- Beginner options trading strategies are easy to learn and easy to understand, which means even beginner options traders can find relatively immediate and meaningful success when they begin trading.

- Option trading is highly flexible, especially when you start trading with different options forms—you can customize options contracts, select strike prices, and even decide expiration dates and cycles for investments.

- There are an array of financial resources, materials, tools, and mobile applications readily available at your fingertips, for little to no cost. In addition, there are a series of high-quality, local brokers and brokerages across the country that are happy to assist, advice, consult, and work for you. (Plus, you have the option to decide whether an online brokerage or human broker is the right financial advisor or tool for your personal financial situation).

Maximizing Your Advantages

We often talk about the benefits and advantages associated with options trading, but then the discussion stops there. There's rarely ever a continued conversation about how we can further branch off from those benefits or maximize our advantages. To help with this oversight, I've included the following section. It's brief, but it'll give the beginner options trader some sort of idea of what you can do within those first 48 hours in order to maximize any of the benefits or advantages you might be receiving from trading options.

- Hire a broker. Think of it this way: an individual trader gets his or her own particular set of benefits and advantages when they trade options, but when you hire a broker or brokerage to work on your "team," you get another whole set of benefits and advantages. Brokers open new doors, so use them to maximize benefits and gain new advantages.

- Utilize sell stops and buy stops. These are automatic actions that your broker or brokerage can handle for you. Sell stops are selling orders that you establish with your broker before pursuing an option or trade. You determine a pre-established price with your broker that indicates when your broker should sell an option. Buy stops work in the opposite manner; they are buy orders. These orders indicate to your broker when he or she should buy an option or stock, once it reaches a price you've previously agreed upon.

- Draft and stick to carefully outlined financial plans to ensure you don't stray in unwanted or unconducive directions. Determining beforehand what risks you're willing to take, and what risks you're not willing to take is extremely helpful during those first 48 hours of trading (when you're still getting a feel for how the market works and moves and how you personally operate as a trader).

Disadvantages

Again, I won't bore you with elaborate explanations of the disadvantages of options trading. Instead, here's another helpful list that clearly outlines why traders might choose to shy away from potential options trading opportunities:

- Options are time-sensitive investments. Yes, you can pick and choose options based on expiration dates, but you'll always be confined to a certain expiration date where you must choose to act, or choose to exit.

- Successful options trading require your attention and time. Without it, you risk losing out on potential profit generating opportunities that come from buying or selling your call or put option at the right, most profitable time.

- Options are without a paper-trail. With stocks and bonds, for example, you'll receive some sort of paper certification regarding your investment. Options are "book-entry" investments, meaning you receive no paper certification that shows your claim to an option or your ownership of an option.

- You're working in the stock market, a highly volatile place where changes occur suddenly and dramatically. You'll need to be on constant alert, or at least hire a broker who will.

- You'll need to be in a somewhat stable financial situation before you can successfully trade. Establishing and frequently adding to some sort of "trading fund" before you begin your options trading endeavors will somewhat remedy an unstable financial situation, however.

Reducing Your Risks

Similar to what we discussed earlier in this chapter, our conversations about the risks and disadvantages of options trading usually, well, end there. We rarely talk about how we can troubleshoot arising problems, or even reduce the degree of financial risks we must take in the first place. Though by no means extensive, I've included a short (but hopefully helpful) preview of the ways in which we can work on doing this with the first 48 hours of trading.

- Trade with this approach in mind: focus your attention and effort toward avoiding risks, rather than securing potential rewards. If you're not convinced, think about this little statistic recorded from a 2013 U.S Trust survey: 60% of millionaire investors place more emphasis on avoiding unnecessary risks than securing potential capital gain.

- Diversify your account. This is essentially just a fancy word for "split up your money to make it safer." When you don't put all of your eggs in one basket, so to speak, you significantly (and technically eliminate) the risk of losing all of your money when one investment opportunity cracks or crumbles.

- Keep a broker or brokerage close by. Beginner traders can benefit greatly from having a highly-trained, experienced financial expert or professional just a phone call or drive away. When trades don't go your way, or you're simply not deriving the benefits you expected from trades, even within that initial 48 hour timeframe, a broker can assist and advise you on how to produce better results and generate more meaningful profit. Or, they can attempt to remedy current, negative financial situations or trades.

Chapter 12: Avoiding Common Mistakes

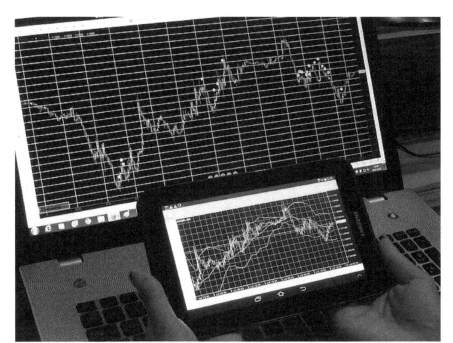

Options are very risky, full stop. There are a lot of places where things can go wrong, and what's more is that it's extremely easy for people newer to the industry to make really simple mistakes that only take a little knowledge and foresight to avoid. The point of this chapter is to analyze these mistakes that a huge number of beginners will make so that you can avoid making them yourself and, hopefully, be a better investor yourself.

Buying cheap call options

Buying calls is absolutely not bad in and of it. But buying cheap calls can be very dangerous, and this is for a multitude of reasons. But before we discuss why it's dangerous, we have to examine why people do this in the first place.

The main reason that people are duped into buying especially cheap call options that are way beyond any sort of reality is, first off, because they're cheap. The low-price tag may present itself as a sort of "gambling" rather than "investment", but even if you're gambling, it's not much of a gamble if there's over an eighty percent likelihood that you'll end up losing the bet.

The other reason that one may be a cheap call option is because it fits a paradigm that they're accustomed to. After all, when you buy a call option, you're just making the prediction that the stock will go up in price, right? And that's the notion that a lot of people make when they're selling **equities**. The whole "buy low, sell high" paradigm absolutely rules the sphere of equity trading. So this is a comfortable paradigm to transfer over to options trading. It doesn't feel too far off from what you know.

However, this is a terrible idea to transfer over, and I'll tell you why: when you buy cheap options, you are buying options which are cheap for a very specific reason. Remember how we talked about things that can affect options premiums? Well, that lesson should apply here. Low cost options contracts are low cost because they aren't expected to pay out well; they're low demand, so the broker doesn't have to ask much in order to make a decent amount off of it.

What's more is that when you buy options on a stock, as we've already discussed, you're already taking into account the timing of a stock hitting a high or a low. Its price will be affected by the likelihood of it going in a specific direction.

In other words, cheap call options are generally cheap because they aren't going to go anywhere, and you'd have to have a miracle and a half to not lose the entirety of your options premium that you paid down, let alone make a profit.

So what can you as a beginner do instead? You should build your equities portfolio and instead **write** calls on stocks that **you own**, rather than **holding** calls on stocks that **others** own. When you do so, what you're basically saying is that you'll sell the stock that you own at the strike price in the option. Since in calls, the price is generally higher than the **strike price**, the risk is minimal. You, as the writer, are simply saying to the holder "if the stock goes up to the strike price, I will sell it at that price, even if it is above the strike price." This means that regardless of what happens, you make a profit, it's just not **quite** as high as it would be otherwise.

This technique is called the "covered call". It's a great way to make a fair amount of early income, and it's relatively safe for you as the writer. The only way that this method could displace your capital is if the stock goes significantly down (more than normal market fluctuations) since the time that you'd invested in it. However, it does limit your ability to sell if your stock goes exponentially up, as it gives you an "earnings" ceiling. But regardless - though you may not become a multimillionaire off of one stock boom, you'll make a steady profit off of selling contracts to your investments.

Moreover, if the market doesn't really go anywhere and just stays flat, and your stock's market price never hits the strike price, you still obtain the premium from the contract buyer for selling him the option in the first place. Meanwhile, you maintain your stock, of course, to repeat the process once more once the expiry date has been reached on a given contract.

So this is a much safer way to get to know the options market as you're just starting out and make a steady amount of income rather than simply going gung-ho on certain out of the money calls. What's more is that instead of putting you in a position to take **risks**, you're putting yourself in a position to be the **risk which others take**. You are in a secure position; if the market stays flat, or goes down a bit; you collect a small premium and maintain your stock. If the market rises to the stock price, you still profit - though maybe not as much as you would have liked to - and can use the resultant capital in order to invest in another stock and repeat the process. The only risk you're undertaking in this scenario is the possibility that your invested capital is devalued. However, the chances of a major crash are much lower, and you still have a certain amount of steady income from the covered calls on the stock.

No plan

This is a critical killer. With anything, it's important to have a "way out" if things don't go your way, and be able to control your emotional reactions should things shift for the worse. However, it's of absolutely paramount importance in the trading game, in a manner which really can't be understated at all. Having a plan is important in every single trade that you'll ever make, and having a sort of "exit" plan is most definitely important, too.

So what do I mean by "have a plan"? It's simple. You need to have a plan in place that you can minimize losses if your trades go for the worse and maximize gains if they go for the better. And this doesn't necessarily mean forming some sort of bizarre clairvoyance for the market and knowing exactly what's going to happen.

Rather, it's about recognizing patterns and developing a finite way for you to react to these patterns. This is absolutely imperative, actually. If you don't do this, then you're going to find yourself taking massive losses waiting for an option to go in the money as you near your expiry date, or you're going to find your options taking turns for the worse because you wanted to wait around and see if a stock would continue to go up.

You need to set up a plan for yourself: what sort of gains will make you happy as a trader when you're on the upside? What is the worst you'll allow things to get on the downside before dodging out? Evaluate how trades have gone wrong before and specifically factor in for those. Do you have a habit of getting a bit greedy and losing good deals because a given stock did a 180 and ended up losing more than you would have gotten otherwise? Do you have a habit of holding onto stocks for too long when they're bad and losing more money than is necessary in the process? Identify those and specifically set up plans for those traits in particular.

Illiquidity

Liquidity essentially means the ease with which a person can buy or sell something without there being a significant change in the price of that thing. This means that there must always be a large amount of active traders within the market. In a mathematical sense, liquidity as a concept represents the likelihood that the following trade will be around the same price as the prior one, preferably with the two trades being of equal price.

Options markets are by their nature less liquid than stock markets are because stock markets operate on a simple notion of equity. You sell a share, you buy a share, that share represents the essential concept of a piece of something bigger, but there's little way to change that share. That share is that share, basically. Options markets, however, offer a variety of different contracts. On options markets, one may buy a long call option, a long put option, a short call option, a short put option, and any variation of options contracts therein. They can buy American style options or British style options. They generally have a lot more variance in both the mechanisms of trade as well as the things which are being traded themselves. Because of this, options markets **are** far less liquid than stock markets, because there's so much more variance for people to account for.

A company which trades constantly is unlikely to be a liquidity issue, regardless of whether you're operating on the stock market or the options market. However, if a company is smaller or has stock which trades far less frequently, then it's much more illiquid.

It follows that if a given stock should be illiquid, because of the different mechanisms at work then the options contracts available to that same company will be even more illiquid. This means that the bid and ask price for options become very artificially distant. This means that a lot of money would be spent in order just to establish a position. (Stock lingo for "buy it"; "clear your position" means to sell stock)

So what can you do to prevent this? The easiest way is to avoid trading illiquid options, simply put. Research every single investment you make very well, and be certain that the interest in the stock is incredibly high. Trading illiquid assets can be a massive setback and cost you far more than you'd make off of it, and it will save you a lot of stress too. There are a huge number of opportunities for good liquid options contracts that are readily available to you.

Trading options can be incredibly difficult. Here, I only put the three most egregious examples which came to mind, but all of them are extremely common and admittedly tempting mistakes that beginner traders will make in the world of options trading. It's important that if you want to grow as a trader, you recognize as many of **other** people's mistakes as you can. If you do so, you're making silently sure that you don't make those same mistakes yourself; in effect making you a far better trader than you would be otherwise.

Conclusion

The next step is to implement all of this. Learn, learn, learn, and at some point take the jump to invest and start learning by experience.

I feel like I need to reiterate this one last time for good measure: options trading is dangerous. It's not something that you can just passively be involved in, and honestly, it's not a good place for any beginning trader to get involved in. It takes a lot of extensive theory and knowledge about exactly the things you're working with, and you're going to find often that you'll be losing instead of gaining -- especially as a beginner trader.

What are the ways to circumvent this? Well, there isn't. The obvious route is to simply go with something more lucrative and less risky. For example, if you just invest in equities and indexes, you can expect something like a six percent growth rate. After all, the economy is growing constantly. Neoliberal economic policies only exacerbate this sense of growth such that if you can actually afford to make a reasonable investment into equities or indexes, you will almost certainly see a positive return on it, albeit a smaller one.

Some time ago, before I devoted myself to studying finances and learning how to be a good investor, driven mainly by an intense interest in the way that the markets ticked and worked and the way that wealth moved around in our economy, a friend shared with me some very pertinent advice: "you're better off investing in yourself than investing in stocks." Since then, that's somewhat resonated.

Investments are called investments for a reason: they're long-term investments intended to accrue a certain amount of revenue over time, and if the company in which you invested does well, you too will benefit from the resultant success of course. That's the nature of investments.

But it's also a very impersonal and unsure way to make money. If you're looking for a get rich quick scheme, this is not it. Investing has a whole lot of upsides and can be a lot of fun and an absolutely crazy ride. But that doesn't mean that it's intended to make you a ton of money. If you're looking for localized investment with high returns, there are better ways to do it, such as learning about making money by affiliate marketing or creating worthwhile content.

The long and short of it is that investing is intended for people who have extra money. It's not intended for people to make extra money. Some just happen to. Most, in fact, do, but it's very, very unlikely that you're going to be the next Warren Buffet because of investment, especially in options trading.

And that goes further to say that if this is really what you want to do, be prepared to lose some money in the process. Options trading are hard to get into as a beginner, and take a fair amount of capital to even get a decent start. However, if you decide that it's what you want to do, here's how I can sum up the path for you going forward.

The first thing is to only even consider doing options trading with your speculative capital. What speculative capital means is money that you can set aside and essentially afford to lose should things go awry. Never, ever invest money that you genuinely need. Before doing any sort of investiture, be certain that you have at least 3 months of emergency savings set up and that you can afford to lose every single cent that you're putting into it. There's not a successful trader that won't tell you this. This isn't to turn you away from investing; it's a very real way to make very real capital gains... if you know what you're doing. But every single worthwhile trader out there will tell you to prepare to lose. Don't ever do anything that puts you in a worse position than you started out in. Only ever invest capital that you do not need.

The second thing is to spend a fair amount of time doing research. Research is ultimately the name of the game in any sort of investing. A part of me feels like that goes without saying, but it should be driven home that it is absolutely the case. Research is the fundamental crux of every decision that happens in the marketplace. It's only by knowing about a company, about its founder and its board and about its upcoming products, by knowing its past history and its marketplace trends, by knowing the trends of the market in general, by knowing what things like beta bid/ask are and how they have an impact on the viability of an options trade, and by knowing in-depth a lot of key concepts on the marketplace that you can even think of becoming a renowned options trader.

The third thing is far less general - you're going to have a much easier time starting out as an options trader if you build a portfolio and then proceed to sell contracts on those options. It will give you a much kinder sandbox with a lot less shards of glass where you can learn the ins and outs of options trading while still being a safe distance away from any real economic harm. Every single new options trader should spend a lot of time doing covered calls until they feel as though they sufficiently know the market and what they're doing and how they have a hand in the market at large.

In the end, if you feel like trading, you absolutely should. I genuinely hope that I've given you enough foundational information such that you can make informed decisions about the things you'll be doing on the market. Options trading, as I said, can be very lucrative if you know what you're doing. My goal in writing this book was to help set you up to know what you're doing.

So if you've made it past all my warnings and second-guess and you've decided that you still definitely want to move forward on options trading, and then what are you waiting for? Go back to one of the brokers we discussed in chapter four and start an account. Does some research before you make a deposit so that you're sure this is the step you want to take, and once you're positive, take the steps you have to get into the game?

Options trading is endlessly fun and rewarding if you find yourself interested in these sort of things, and I can't help but feel like you'll very much enjoy your time spent doing it if you've made it this far into this book. So go for it!

CPSIA information can be obtained
at www.ICGtesting.com
Printed in the USA
LVHW080533250121
677402LV00010B/353